PORTRAIT OF ORKNEY

PORTRAIT OF ORKNEY

GEORGE MACKAY BROWN

With photographs by Werner Forman

1981 · THE HOGARTH PRESS · London

By the same Author

*

Poems
Fishermen with Ploughs
Loaves and Fishes
The Year of the Whale
Winterfold
Selected Poems

Short Stories
A Calendar of Love
A Time to Keep
Hawkfall
The Sun's Net

Play
A Spell for Green Corn

Novels
Greenvoe
Magnus

Essays
An Orkney Tapestry (Gollancz)
Letters from Hamnavoe (Gordon Wright Publishing)
Under Brinkie's Brae (Gordon Wright Publishing)

For Children
The Two Fiddlers
Pictures in the Cave
Six Lives of Fankle the Cat

Published by
The Hogarth Press Ltd
40 William IV Street
London WC2N 4DF

*

Clarke, Irwin & Co. Ltd
Toronto

*British Library Cataloguing
in Publication Data*
Brown, George Mackay
    Portrait of Orkney.
    1. Orkney Islands – History
    I. Title
    941.13′2   DA880.06
    ISBN 0-7012-0513-X   *8/89 10 ⁰⁰*

Text © George Mackay Brown 1981
Photographs © Werner Forman 1981

Colour illustrations originated by
Keene Engraving Co. Ltd., London

Printed in Great Britain by
BAS Printers Limited, Over Wallop, Hampshire

In Memoriam
Edwin and Willa Muir

The publishers gratefully acknowledge the support given by the members of the Occidental North Sea Consortium: Occidental of Britain, Inc.; Getty Oil (Britain) Limited; Thomson North Sea Limited; and Allied (North Sea) Limited, for the production of this book. They and the author also acknowledge permission to reproduce copyright material as follows: Extract from *The Man on my Back* by Eric Linklater, reprinted by permission of A. D. Peters; 'Childhood' from *Collected Poems* by Edwin Muir, reprinted by permission of Faber & Faber and of Oxford University Press, Inc., New York; 'Celestial Kinsmen' from *Orkney Variants and Other Poems* by Robert Rendall, reprinted by permission of Mr R. P. Rendall.

Contents

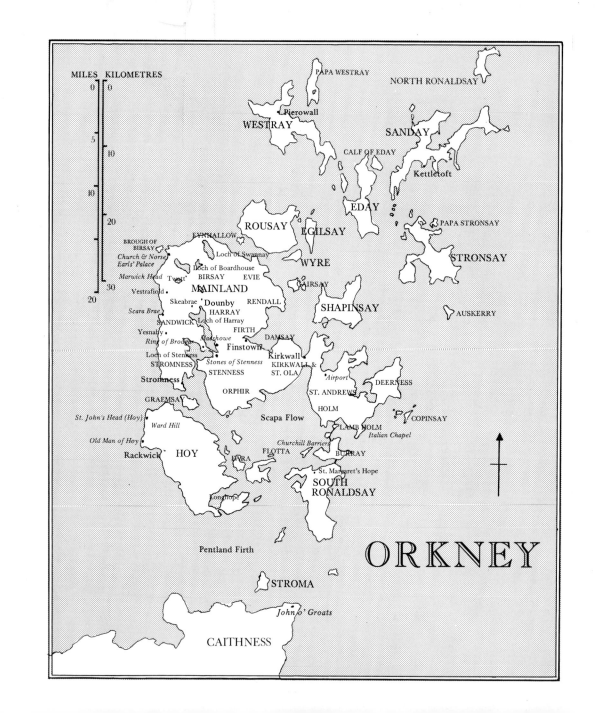

MILES KILOMETRES

PAPA WESTRAY

NORTH RONALDSAY

Pierowall

WESTRAY

SANDAY

CALF OF EDAY

Kettletoft

EDAY

ROUSAY

EGILSAY

PAPA STRONSAY

BROUGH OF
BIRSAY

EYNHALLOW

WYRE

Loch of Swannay

STRONSAY

Church & Norse
Earls' Palace

Loch of Boardhouse

Marwick Head   Twatt'   BIRSAY   EVIE

MAINLAND

GAIRSAY

Vestrafiold

RENDALL

SHAPINSAY

Skeabrae   Dounby

AUSKERRY

Scara Brae

HARRAY

SANDWICK   Loch of Harray

Yesnaby

FIRTH

Ring of Brodgar   Maeshowe

DAMSAY

Finstown

Loch of Stenness

Kirkwall

DEERNESS

STROMNESS   Stones of Stenness

KIRKWALL &
ST. OLA

'Airport

STENNESS

Stromness

ORPHIR

ST. ANDREWS

GRAEMSAY

HOLM

COPINSAY

St. John's Head (Hoy)

Ward Hill

Scapa Flow

LAMB HOLM

Old Man of Hoy

Italian Chapel

Rackwick   HOY

Churchill Barriers

FLOTTA   BURRAY

FARA

St. Margaret's Hope

Longhope

SOUTH
RONALDSAY

Pentland Firth

ORKNEY

STROMA

John o' Groats

CAITHNESS

People 1

THE PEOPLE of Orkney today are a mingled weave. Over the winter fires, when we are not watching television, some of us like to think of ourselves as 'sons of the Vikings'. To go into the history of these mediaeval pirates and reivers is not such an edifying experience. No doubt the Norsemen who settled in the islands, and farmed and traded and fished, form an important strain in the modern Orcadian. Especially in the North Isles, you can see tall fair-haired blue-eyed men and women who seem to be 'typically Scandinavian'.

But our modern blood springs from many sources. What ingenious folk built the brochs? Who were the Picts? *Orkneyinga Saga* is silent about them – you might think the sagamen would have delighted in telling how the first Norsemen outwitted and destroyed the Picts, and made of their keeps wide strewments of stone. But there is nothing. Perhaps what happened is that there was slow infiltration from the east over centuries – a storm-driven longship, gaunt-faced traders, silent night-shrouded raiders, even a tentative settler in this island and that – until in the end the new culture, laws, ways of sailing and farming took over completely. If that was the way of it, there is probably as much Pictish blood in us as Norse. Even if the conquest was sudden and violent, we may be sure that the girls were not despised.

The blond word-man in the first death-ship said, 'We removed stone from stone, on a western beach.' Sigurd the skipper said, 'I think we can build a hall and a few proper farms here. . . .' Sigurd said later, 'Take the best of the women down to the ship. . . .'

The sources go much further back. No doubt, such are the blood's intricate interweavings, some of our remote ancestors were at the building of Brodgar and Skara Brae. They dragged the huge stones from Vestrafiold and trundled them all the way to the dark moor between the lochs. They manhandled monoliths for the master-masons of Maeshowe. What kind of people they were – their laws and music and language – are utterly lost. But it seems they saw life not as a brief line, birth-to-death, but as a circle which has neither beginning nor end.

THE NEW CHIEF : QUANTERNESS

First was given, with new edges,
A breast cut
Deep, for a welling of light.

The moon-thirled women
Turned wheels
All about him: wool, milk, stone.

The chief came, hooded,
To a red stone marked OX. Thereafter
Furrow and fire were ours.

(Who chose this man? Roots
Cried, stars sang,
Gulls wrote a name in the air and in water.)

Yesterday he idled
Grass-biting, a herdboy. Now
He rules, horned, from the centre.

As we are drawn
To snow and eclipse, his hand
Makes the sign of the sun.

He died one shearing time,
Webs of winter on him.
He returns, lissom, a boy again, with leaf and lamb.

Were there other more mysterious ancestors still, shadows upon darkness? For them, primitive and short-lived as they were, the land and sea, after the retreat of the ice, must have seemed a new marvellous place, swarming with plants and animals and birds and fish that were more their kin than their prey (though, to live, they were forced to hunt them).

But finally and irrefutably, it was the Norse laws and culture that triumphed. Because they were masterly story-tellers, and delighted in that art in all its purity, we have in *Orkneyinga Saga* a matchless record of the way their earls and great men and women lived and thought. They delighted too in the intricate web of kinship; some of the sagas begin with a long formal account, going many generations back, of what lineage the chief characters in the story to be told were begotten. This gift has come down in all its essentials to certain modern Orkney men and women; you have simply to name a person in the presence of these 'kin-redders', and they will immediately surround that name with cousins, step-brothers, uncles, grandfathers: the web, fixed deep in time, may span the world nowadays from Vancouver to New South Wales. If it sounds like a dry art, there are in every family certain incidents and involvements to give it spice.

The Norsemen had hardly taken over when, naturally, their chiefs were drawn into the orbits of Scottish high society. Whether we like it or not, the greatest of the Orkney earls, Thorfinn the Mighty, was a cousin of King Macbeth of Scotland. Thorfinn did not look at all like 'a son of the Vikings':

> He was of all men the tallest and strongest; he was ugly; he had black hair, a large nose and a rather dark complexion. He had enormous energy, and he desired above all things riches and good fame. . . .
>
> (*Orkneyinga Saga*)

The Scottish influence grew over the generations; it was natural, Norway was far away eastward, and the growing kingdom of Scotland lay just across the Pentland Firth. Yet the language of the Norsemen was such a vivid inheritance to this increasingly mingled race that it was remembered here and there, in croft and noust, until late in the eighteenth century. There was a sufficient scattering of the old words only fifty years ago for Dr Hugh Marwick to put together a dictionary of them, *The Orkney Norn*.

What the *Saga* does not tell us is what life was like for the common people of Orkney and Shetland between the eighth and thirteenth centuries. There is one glimpse only, among heroic battle shouts, intrigues, burnings, festive songs in the high hall; that is the moving story of how Earl Rognvald fished dangerous

A standing stone in the Ring of Brodgar, and Hoy across the loch

waters with a Shetland crofter, and how afterwards the shore women laughed as their hooded lord slipped and fell in the seaweed. . . .

But there they lived and drudged, generation after generation, in their little 'toonships' beside the sea, or on the loch-shore, breaking the soil with primitive shares, berated by their women (the women of the north have seemed to be always more powerful characters than any other women in the world), reaping the sudden silver harvest and the slow golden harvest, hedged in by dark supernatural powers, hoarding a bit of butter and a few dried fish to pay the earl or the bishop his rent.

> *I rent and till a patch of dirt*
> *Not much bigger than my coat.*
> *I keep a cow and twelve swine*
> *And some sheep and a boat.*
> > *Drudgings, stone.*
>
> *The name of my wife is Hild.*
> *Hild has a bitter tongue.*
> *She makes passable butter and ale.*
> *Her mouth brims and brims with bairnsong.*
> > *Driftings, stone.*
>
> *What's winter? A thousand stars,*
> *Shrinkings of snow, an empty pail.*
> *All summer I go, a drenched ox*
> *Between the plough and the flail.*
> > *Drudgings, stone. . . .*

Pictish symbol stone from Broch of Burrian, Harray (*Tankerness House Museum*)

Yet the drudgery and the drift were brightly starred with festivals and junketings: Yule, Beltane, Johnsmas, Lammas, Hallowe'en, Saints' days. And such natural events as birth, marriage, death were not allowed to pass into oblivion without music, ale, dancing feet. To see an ancient Orkney wedding must have been an entrancing experience: the long column of countryfolk, led by a fiddler, wending its way two by two between the bride's house and the minister's manse, and back again after the ceremony, that one white splash among the sombre homespun. Then, in the barn, the drinking and mirth and dancing went on till beyond cockcrow. Before the revellers went home they drank, in a sunwise circle, from the bride's cog – a round wooden vessel filled with hot ale, spices, whisky. . . . Often the wedding celebrations went on for days, as if these folk were reluctant (and who shall blame them?) to return once more to the uncertain wheel of agriculture.

BRIDE SONG

In the barn, fiddle and flute
Are at odds, the dancing feet
Slower and heavier stamp,
The ale sinks low in the jar.
I unlatch a secret door.
'Come quickly. I've turned the cold sheet.
I have put
Only a little oil in the lamp.'

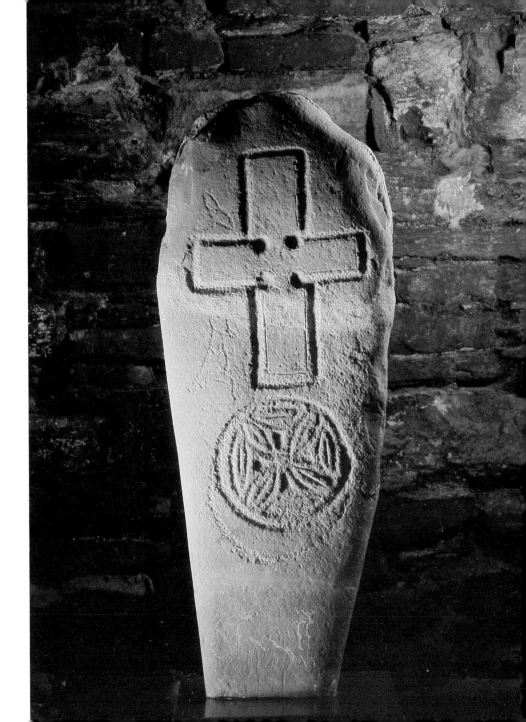

Early Christian stone, Papa Westray
(*Tankerness House Museum*)

They were so humble and anonymous that originally they had only the names given them in baptism, and if it was necessary to particularise some person more closely, they called him or her 'Peter's son' or 'Magnus's dottor', or 'Thorfinn's son'. So the surnames changed with every generation: to a hunter of genealogies it is impossibly confusing. There must be records of a fairly definite time when everyone, possibly in order that the earl might have a more precise roll-call of the governed (for fiscal or other reasons), was compelled to take a fixed surname. The Orcadians solved the situation simply: they called themselves by the district or parish or island where they lived at the time – Marwick, Linklater, Halcrow, Heddle, Firth, Harra, Corston, Corrigall, Cursiter, Rendall, Baikie, Isbister, Twatt.... (Some argue that these names were given to families who had removed to another island or parish.) It is possible to argue that Orcadians with these 'district names' are older truer islanders than certain other families like Spence, Sinclair, Sutherland, Brown, Muir, Tait, who must have drifted in (from Scotland mainly) over the generations; it is probable that the infamous Stuart earls, so artistically sensitive but such bad governors, brought retinues of Scotsmen north with them into the islands. But the whole question of genealogy is such a tangle that it is foolish to say or conjecture how much native blood flows in a man's veins; and, as we've seen, Orkney blood was from the beginning a sampling and a mixing from many wells.

It is arguably good for a people that they have variety in their ancestry. Most of us have seen what horrors were loosed on the earth only a few decades ago in the name of racial purity. Royal and noble families who tried, in past centuries, to maintain their blood untainted, had to endure for such folly incurable ailments of body and mind.

No doubt, in certain isolated parts of Orkney, there was inbreeding that resulted in similar weaknesses. In the eighteenth century and earlier, it's said, a 'toonship' or a district resented it if a young man from another place came courting there; everything was done to discourage the suitor.

But one constant in Orkney history is the infusion of new blood, from this distant airt and that. Shipwrecks were common in former times. Did one of the Armada ships blunder against an Orkney coast? There are traditions of shipwrecked sailors from other lands, staying on and marrying local girls. There is the very moving story of a ship – either she was called 'Archangel' or she was out of that port – bound from Russia to America (loaded with immigrants, possibly) going ashore on Westray. Only one child, an anonymous boy, was saved from the wreck. That is why there was a family called Angel in Westray until recently.

When the Orkneymen, like their Norse forbears, sailed north-west in the nineteenth century after whales, or to work at the Hudson's Bay Company's fur posts, they did not remain celibate. Many of them loved their Indian wives well enough to take them back home, once they had earned enough money to rent a croft or a little farm in the islands.

The two world wars saw huge influxes of soldiers, sailors, airmen from all over Britain; and, as the war went on, from further afield. To an already complex bloodstream were added these exotic strains. No one shall say that the Orkney people were soiled or spoiled by the admixture. Indeed, one of the very gratifying things about young Orkney folk, however descended, is the perennial love they have for the islands. Many of them are forced of necessity to make their livings elsewhere; whenever an opportunity comes, they are true as salmon to the native streams.

Mermaids on a doorway
of St Magnus Cathedral

Is there a typical Orkney face? There are farmers and their wives at the Dounby Agricultural Show with apple-cheeks and ready laughter and shy careful speech. There are the fair-haired blue-eyed laconic fishermen from the islands. Islanders who do not belong to Kirkwall see in the faces of the capital lineaments not discernible in the outlying parishes and islands: an alertness (for want of a better word) springing perhaps from centuries of commercialism and close-knittedness. Stromnessians, too, are said to have their own speech and cast of countenance. 'The Orkney face' contains within itself great variety. All that can be safely said is that the earth and skies and sea that people live among get worked at last into the flesh and bone.

> *Many masks merge in an island face,*
> *Pict, Norseman, Scot,*
> *Salt wanderers, tremulous first-comers*
> *After the ice broke.*
> *Face of the countryman, strength of loam in it.*
> *Faces of fishermen, sailor: the eyes*
> *Level as horizons.*

There was a minister in Kirkwall in the late seventeenth century who wrote an enchanting book about the islands and their people. The English language was so rich then that merely to put pen to paper, it seems, begot felicities and delights. (We tend, increasingly, to speak and write more like computers than

Tombstone in St Magnus
Cathedral, Kirkwall:
wife of the minister and
historian, James Wallace

A country shop, Evie

like imaginative beings.) Rev James Wallace, unlike the Cromwellian soldier who a few years earlier wrote a filthy ill-natured poem about Orkney and Orcadians, had a sweet nature and a perceptive eye. What he wrote about the islanders of three centuries ago is largely true today. Whether he was an Orkneyman or not, there is no doubt, judging from his beautiful prose, that he was under the spell of the islands. I can do no better than to make a little anthology of his remarks.

The People here are generally Civil, sagacious, Circumspect, and Piously Inclined. Though *Boethius* reports them to be great Drunkards. . . . Yet now it is not soo: For though they use strong Ale and Beer (the nature of the Climate requiring strong Liquor) yet generally they are sober, and Temperate, but withal much given to Hospitality and Feasting, very Civil and Liberal in their Entertaining of Strangers. . . .

The People are generally personable and Comelie. . . . The Women are Lovely, and of a Beautiful Countenance, and are very Broodie and apt for Generation, One *Marjorie Bimbister* in the Parish of *Evie*, was in the year 1683 brought to bed of a Male Child, in the sixtie-third year of her Age. . . .

By reason of the Temperance of their Dyet, and wholesomeness of the Air, the People usually Live to a good Age. A Man in the parish of *Ham*, died not many years since, who had Lived upwards of four-score years with his Wife in a Married estate. There is also a Gentleman yet living in *Stronsa*, who was begotten of his Father when he was a hundred years of age, and did live till he saw this same man's Children.

All speak English, with a good Accent, only some of the common People among themselves speak *Norse* or the old *Gottish Language*, which they have derived to them, either from the *Pights*, who first Peopled this Countrey, or from the *Danes* and *Norvegians*, in whose possession it once was.

A Flotta interior.
The paraffin lamp is a
rarity in Orkney now.

2 Land

THE PLACE before was boggy and thick with stones; but in a short time Earl Magnus's goodness gleamed Godward with such radiance that there came up abundant greeness in the place where he had been killed.

This miracle of fertility out of barrenness, the desert blossoming as the rose, is a kind of parable of Orkney agriculture. In four thousand years what was originally dark moor – stone and bog everywhere, except where blown shell sand had sweetened the beach-girding soil – has come to wear everywhere the green coat of fertility. Half way up the hills go the plough and the reaper. Sometimes you get the feeling that nowadays too much has been reclaimed; the old wild places, so beautiful in their own way, have been pushed too far back.

> *What would the world be, once bereft*
> *Of wet and wildness? Let them be left,*
> *O let them be left, wildness and wet;*
> *Long live the weeds and the wilderness yet.*
>
> (G. M. HOPKINS)

Seeking fertile places to settle in: that is what took successive races to Orkney, even (we presume) before the time of agriculture. Sea and lochs and sky teemed with fish and fowl for the hunters; even the shore at ebb-tide was generous.

The first Norsemen to settle peaceably – there had been plenty of red-handed pirates in the preceding centuries from east-over-sea – planned their farms (the 'bu' of the chief) in watered slopes and valleys fronting the sea, like Marwick or Cairston; and there they began the slow arduous business of drainage and digging and quickening.

> *Hills for bees to be hived,*
> *Beasts kept, a cod-hungry boat,*
> *A comfort of fire in the crofts.*
> *We furled sails, set firm our feet,*
> *Stone laid against stone. . . .*
> *Dreamed I that darkness*
> *Of horse, harp, a hallowed harvest.*

It proved to be a kindly soil, and the country men and women of Orkney have from the beginning been hard workers. It is said that the neolithic inhabitants of Orkney, who existed round the howes of the dead that were so important to them, hardly lived beyond the age of thirty, and their housed bones are twisted with arthritis. In the eighteenth century an Orkneyman was old and bent with labour by the time he was fifty (but perhaps he was healthier than other countrymen who had moved into the new industrial cities; certainly his life had a meaningful pattern, he was bound to the slow fruitful cycle of the year, seed time to harvest). Nowadays Orcadians are materially better off than they have ever been, they are healthy and generally long-lived; but,

together with the hard back-breaking toil, much of the old mystery and fulfilment of agricultural life is no longer there. It has vanished with the horse.

The horse at the shore
Casks of red apples, skull, a barrel of rum

The horse in the field
Plough, ploughman, gulls, a furrow, a cornstalk

The horse in the peatbog
Twelve baskets of dark fire

The horse at the pier
Letters, bread, paraffin, one passenger, papers

The horse at the Show
Ribbons, raffia, high bright hooves

The horse in the meadow
A stallion, a russet gale, between two hills

The horse at the burn
Quenching a long flame in the throat

The biggest island of Orkney is called nowadays, insipidly, Mainland; but in Norse times and probably long afterwards on the tongues of country folk it was Hrossey, 'the island of the horse'. The horse was the animal that the farmer used and loved best of all. Without the labour of ox and horse he could hardly have stitched those fertile patches of oats and barley and grass on to the original bleakness. From some of the more barren islands around, where men depended on creel and hook more than the plough, the big island with its many-coloured fields must have seemed, truly, 'the horse island'.

Our isle is oyster-gray.
That patched coat
Is the Island of Horses.

The tractor has long taken over from the horse. There are still old farmers alive who never forgot the strong bond between horse and man; they kept their faithful beasts round the farm until they died of age. We may imagine how some of them felt – and the saddlers and blacksmiths too – when the first tractor stuttered and stank across a field.

The horsemen are red in the stable
With whisky and wrath.
The petrol-drinker is in the hills.

But in general Orcadians took to the machines – cars, tractors, boat-engines, reapers – with as much passion as they will ever allow themselves. The fact that the life blood of the machine – oil – is massively stored under the sea to the east is a source of satisfaction to most modern Orkneymen; though they say little about it, one way or the other. Those who have reservations are the environmentalists, the guardians of the heritage; and they tend to be more passionate and articulate.

Slowly the original 'bu' farms grew and begot other farms as more and more of the hill was unlocked by the plough: the 'setters', 'bisters', 'brecks', 'quholms', in all their combinations and varieties. The Norse name-givers were strictly factual – the farm names describe, coldly, the situation of the enclosure, or some outstanding feature or peculiarity of it, or (perhaps for want of any special characteristic) the farm is called by the name of the first farmer. . . . Right up to Orkney's 'agricultural revolution' of

14th century farmhouse at Kirbister, Birsay

only a few generations ago, the cultivated land of a district was enclosed by a turf dyke; beyond the wall ranged the herds of cow and sheep and swine; and so the rigs of bere and oat inside were left all summer to take the sun's burnish. But sometimes, because there were too many people in a 'tunship', the dyke had to be breached so that a patch of dung-fertilised hill land beyond could be put under the plough, and these little enclosures were called 'quoys'. The element 'quoy' is probably the commonest among Orkney farm names.

Coldly descriptive the original farm names were; but now, in the long perspective of time, they have a fascination for all Orkney-lovers. Nowadays, when new houses are built, all kinds of fanciful inappropriate ludicrous names are bestowed on them.

> *The old crofts ride a green hill surge,*
> *Long arks, men and beasts under one roof.*
> *The new bungalows,*
> *Will they be there at the dove's return?*

Hugh Marwick's *Orkney Farm Names* is a brilliant exploration of the subject. Another fine book, about the vanished ways of agriculture in Orkney is John Firth's *Reminiscences of an Orkney Parish*, which has lately been reprinted.

Hard and anxious the lives of country folk must have been, almost up to the present day. Yet they did not deny themselves festival and fiddle and dance, whenever the time of year for those celebrations came round. The twelve days of Yule (Christmas)

Last of the old peat fires, Kirbister.
The smoke escapes through a
hole in the roof.

Stone nook-bed, Kirbister

were full of elaborate and beautiful ceremonies carried out by the farmer in his own house and outbuildings and fields. The farmer on the morning of the Nativity put a candle in a cow's skull and by the light of this lantern fed his beasts in the byre with more fodder than usual. There is rich beautiful age-old symbolism in what was happening – the fruitful interaction of bread, death, new light. . . . All the ritual element is out of life nowadays, and we are the poorer for it.*

No longer are the midsummer bonfires lit on the summit of every hill in Orkney: a salutation to the sun, an entreaty for the sun's light and kindling to visit this parish and that island, so that, between now and harvest, there would be no blight in the ripening oats. When the fire was at its height, each crofter would light from it his own private torch, and carry it alone through his steading and fields. Till dawn came – and at that time of year sunset and dawn kept the one lamp glowing just under the northern horizon – there was eating and drinking and dancing, and the young men leapt like heroes through the flames.

We have had to give up a great deal of the richly ceremonial in order to arrive at our present state of security and affluence. Who nowadays would give up his car, his colour TV, his holiday in the sun, to dance round a fire on midsummer's eve, or greet the animals on a Yule morning with the 'light-out-of-death' lantern?

*The ceremonies recorded are from Shetland, but the two island groups were so close, in geography and race and culture, that Orkney must have shared them.

Retired seaman sitting on
a box-bed, the kind of bed,
wooden and with shutters,
which was used by everybody
until fairly recently.
Note the telescope.

Croft interior, Flotta,
a stone's throw from
an oil terminal

Orkney's agricultural revolution began nearly two centuries ago, and it has completely altered the appearance of the islands, and their prosperity; and perhaps the very nature of the people.

It began when the lairds suddenly found themselves poor, with the collapse of the kelp trade. No longer did the smoke of burning seaweed rise in summer from the stone pits along the shore. What, at all events, had countrymen to do with such artificial trade, subject to all the fluctuations of world commerce?

The landlords *had* to make their acres pay, or else live in crumbling poverty-stricken mansions.

Like the tide coming in, here fast, there reluctantly, the land improvements took place. (One of the greatest obstacles to improvement was the conservative attitude of the crofters themselves; to those who have won so precarious a foothold in time, any change must seem likely to be for the worse.) Enclosures, rotation of crops, division of the common land, introduction of new breeds of cattle, sheep, horses, the bringing in by the lairds of progressive farmers from the south to manage the large home farms – these gradually accomplished a change for the better. At the end of the nineteenth century there was 250 per cent more arable land in Orkney than at the beginning.

Even so, the situation of the crofters and small tenants continued to be precarious. They were at the mercy of the lairds, both as regards their rent and their period of tenure (they could be put out of their holdings at very short notice; they had no inducement to improve their steadings or widen the patch of green round about).

Peat hill. Each household in a parish with a peat bog has its own strip.

An act of parliament of 1886 altered everything in their favour. Fair rents were imposed – arrears of rent reduced or wiped out. They were secure from sudden arbitrary eviction. If for some reason they did leave their holdings, the landlord had to compensate them adequately for any improvements they had carried out.

The position of the lairds was very much weakened by the same act. Slowly, the large estates (or most of them) were split up and sold to the small farmers and crofters who now occupied their own independent holdings. Henceforth they were completely independent of all but weather, pest, and the laws of supply and demand.

Still, here and there on the islands, are the 'big houses' of the lairds. They have fine situations; some of the older houses are very beautiful; some of the Victorian ones more vulgar and brash.

The Crofters Holdings (Scotland) Act of 1886 was the basis of Orkney's present agricultural prosperity.

Slowly the green encroached on heath and moor. Larger sturdier sheep and cattle moved on the new fertile hillsides.

In the first sixty years of this century the number of cattle has doubled, and the number of sheep has more than doubled. (And we should not forget that the sheep and the cattle were quite other, in size and yield, than the miserable 'bestial' described by Rev George Barry in 'Nature Anthology' in the present book.) It was otherwise alas, with the poor horse. It came, because of the machines, within an ace of 'a final solution'. Is it illusion, or are there more horses in our summer fields than there were two decades ago? Like the horses in Edwin Muir's great poem of that name, perhaps these faithful animals – in spite of the ill that has been done them – refuse to break the ancient treaty with men.

It has been found, too, that grass crops are more suited to our soil and climate than the traditional oats, bere, barley. While the new green of grass takes over, increasingly, from the bog and hill – and this crop, at the times of ripeness and cutting, makes

marvellous vivid strips of colour – the number of farms and farmers decreases. The tendency is for smaller farms to be gradually absorbed into bigger units; and the government actively encourages this thinning out with what's called a 'copper handshake' to the small farmer who surrenders his few acres. Increasing mechanisation has made this development unavoidable.

Other improvements have been the spread of electricity all over the countryside, so that now only the most remote places are without it (but not for much longer), and various water schemes that have done away with the laborious getting of water from well or burn, several times a day. (It can be argued, of course, that the more easily available the necessities of life are, the less we appreciate them: water on tap is at last only a tasteless liquidity.) But most Orkney country-folk still appreciate their fire: with their thews and sweat they dig the peat from the bog as their remote ancestors did. Perhaps if coal and electricity were not so expensive, the peat-bogs would be empty of workers in early summer too. Meantime we still have, all over the Orkney countryside at all seasons, the enchanting aroma of peat-smoke at the open doors.

In two centuries Orkney agriculture has come a long way. Yet strong links with the past endure; in some farms the same families have tilled the earth continuously for nine hundred years; and in others for periods almost as long.

To see the Orkney country folk in relaxed mood, go to the Agricultural Show in Dounby, where the three parishes meet, in early August. The sense of imminent harvest is in the air. All around the village of Dounby, the fields are green, or heavy with burnish. On display, in a single square field, are all the finest produce of the Orkney farms; powerful ponderous bulls, silky rich-uddered cows, sheep marvellously fleeced, cocks that give the sun a rousing salute every few minutes. In the marquees are dispensed the produce of the farm kitchens – bannocks, scones, rhubarb jam, pancakes, buns of every kind. If you would enjoy the Orkney farmers in the flavour of a unique humour and in their miracles of understatement, the whisky tent is the place to go: you are experiencing immemorial country flavours, listening to the authentic tongue-music of a thousand years and more. 'A fair field full of folk' – the Dounby Show is a democratic assembly; every kind and condition of Orkney men and women are there: in addition to the farmers and the farm folk – laird, clerks, mechanics, shop-keepers, tourists, 'the professional classes', babies, white-beards, fair-ground men, drunks – a tumultuous throng, a gay surging patchwork. For that one bright day in the busy year, it seems that all the people of Orkney have come together to wonder and to celebrate.

Binscarth: one of the 'big houses'

City and Royal Burgh of Kirkwall: the seal
(*Tankerness House Museum*)

A fair cargo, south bound,
with care and despatch
(*Tankerness House Museum*)

21 Ankers
½ Ditto

SHIPPED, by the Grace of God, in good Order and well Conditioned, by *George Taylor of Kirkwall Orkney* in and upon the good Ship called The *Brigantine Elizabeth of Kirkwall* whereof is Master, under God for this present Voyage *William Wood* and now riding at Anchor in the *Kirkwall Road* and, by God's Grace, bound for *the Port of Leith in the Frith of Forth* to say, the Quantity and number of

Twenty One whole ankers and Four half Ankers Foreign Geneva being ~~Marked and~~ Numbred as in the Margin; and are to be delivered in the like good Order and well Conditioned, at the aforesaid Port of *Leith* (the Danger of the Seas only excepted) unto *the said George Taylor*

or to *his* Assigns, he or they paying Freight for the said Goods *according to agreement*

with Primage and Average accustomed. **In Witness** whereof, the Master or Purser of the said Ship hath Affirmed to *Three* Bills of Lading, all of this Tenor and Date; the one of which *three* Bills being accomplished, the other *two* to stand void: And so God send the good Ship to her desired Port in Safety. Amen. **Dated** in *Kirkwall this 11th day of July 1794*

William Wood

Kirkwall 3

THE 'KIRK' part of Kirkwall is not St Magnus Cathedral, but an earlier church dedicated to St Olaf, a few stones of which still stand in a close off Bridge Street. 'Wall' is in fact a corruption of 'voe' (bay). Pedants and map-makers wreaked havoc in our place names at that very sensitive period when place names were becoming fixed. One went so far as to call the main island 'Pomona', which no Orcadian before or since has used; except that one delectable hostelry in Finstown bears the name.

Kirkwall was first mentioned in *Orkneyinga Saga* when the first Earl Rognvald (Brusison) had a house or a hall there. Rognvald must have been a lucky name to bear; this Rognvald Brusison was as attractive and accomplished in his way as the second Earl Rognvald (Kolson). But both died suddenly and violently.

This first Rognvald had the ill-luck to fall out with the man who ruled Orkney jointly with him: his uncle Earl Thorfinn, who was probably the most talented governor ever to rule the islands – Thorfinn's sovereignty extended deep into Scotland, and as far as the Hebrides and Man. Aided by his friend the King of Norway, Earl Rognvald came suddenly on Thorfinn at his hall in Orphir and put torches to it. Among the ashes and charred bones next morning it was presumed that Thorfinn lay. In fact he had taken his wife Ingibiorg in his arms and broken through the smoke and flames, and rowed to Caithness in a small boat.

Assuming that now he was sole lord of Orkney, the young earl with some of his men set out in a boat for the little island of Papa Stronsay. It was the midwinter of 1046. They intended to buy malt for the Yule brewing. Behind him in Kirkwall he left the warriors loaned him by the King in the east: an elite corps. The house in Papa Stronsay was surrounded in the night and set on fire. The earl, garbed like a priest, leapt over the heads of the besiegers, but his little dog, trying to protect him at the shore, barked frantically and drew Thorfinn's burners. They put their daggers into him and made an end: the rocks were red with seaweed and blood.

Thorfinn and his men returned to Kirkwall in Rognvald's boat. Down to the shore came the Norwegian bodyguard to greet their friend, unarmed. There and then they were set upon and slaughtered – all but one man who was given leave to take that piece of new-minted history back to the King in Bergen.

Thus, violently, the story of Kirkwall begins. In the centuries that followed, the growing town was to see other acts of violence: the siege of the castle, murder in the high street, the hanging and burning of sheep thief and witch. Nowadays all that 'wild wark' (as they say in Orkney) is contained in an unique football game played each Christmas Day and New Year's Day between the 'uppies' and the 'doonies'. It is an anarchical game, with no rules or set number of players: back and fore the mostly invisible 'ba'' is hustled by the closely-meshed teams, until sooner or later it is flung into the sea (a 'doonie' victory) or brought to a wall in the Laverock (an 'uppie' gain). Once, fancifully, I wrote a piece about the origin of the game: how a Yule-tide squabble in the fifteenth century between earl's men (down-the-gates) and bishop's men (up-the-gates) led to a young dandy having his head cut off: whereupon both sides tried desperately to get hold

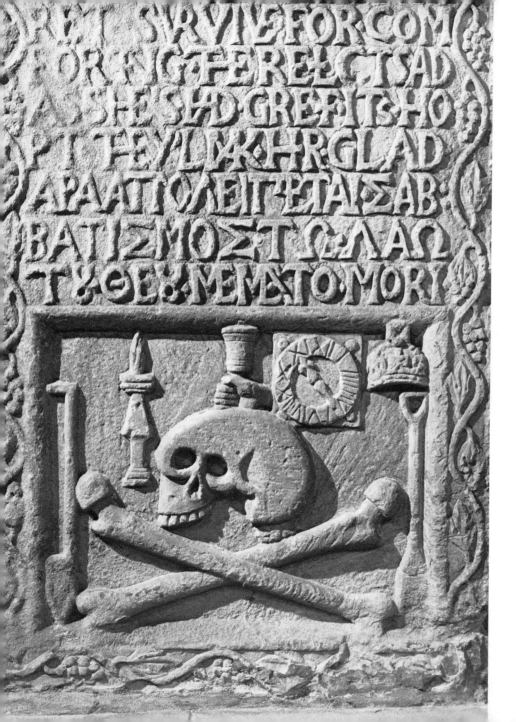

of it, one lot to bring it to the bishop as proof of murder, the other mob to hustle and bury the incriminating thing deep in the sea. . . . But probably the Ba' game is much older: it may be a dramatised myth – the forces of winter and summer, heather and tilth, ice and fire, struggling to possess the sun.

It is easy to see why the first Rognvald chose Kirkwall to build his hall. One glance at the map shows how almost exactly Kirkwall lies at the heart of Orkney – at the point of intersection between North Isles and South Isles, East Mainland and West Mainland. It had the advantage too of having a fine lagoon (now called the Peerie Sea, and much shrunken from its former bounds) where ships could shelter at any season. Men coming and going about their business, by sea or land, were likely to pass in or near Kirkwall: a market town, sooner or later, was bound to take root there. For an earl it must have been the ideal administrative centre.

And yet the great Earl Thorfinn who had Rognvald done to death in the Papa Stronsay ebb chose to rule from Birsay in the north-west of Mainland (some say his palace was on the little steep green tidal island called Brough of Birsay). There too the Bishop had his little cathedral kirk. Perhaps the great earl associated Kirkwall too much with Rognvald, and so turned his back on it. Birsay, of course, is a beautiful place, perhaps the most pleasant and fruitful region in all Orkney. The next three generations of earls – Paul and Erlend, Hakon and Magnus, Harald and Paul – continued, we presume, to rule from Birsay or Orphir or elsewhere. Meantime the little market village

'Awaits alike the inevitable hour. . .'
tomb in St Magnus Cathedral

continued to grow. There men exchanged news and bits of silver, dried fish and sacks of corn, Irish linen and Norse timber. There the little kirk of Saint Olaf gave sweet tongue with its bell on a feast day.

It was the eye of the second Earl Rognvald, St Magnus's nephew, that picked on 'kirk-bay' village to be his capital. It was he who ordered the building of the great cathedral of St Magnus that still stands almost unscathed – a miracle when one thinks of the tempests of history it has weathered. The first blocks of red sandstone from quarries near and far were being set in place when Rognvald Kolson departed with fifteen ships on his great crusade of 1151–54. When he got back from Jerusalem, Constantinople, Rome, the great stone rose would be breaking from its bud. There, in a huge pillar, the bones of St Magnus were brought from Birsay and ceremonially immured.

The history of Kirkwall – rich and tumultuous for so small a city – has been marvellously and meticulously recorded in a fine book published locally at the end of last century – Hossack's *Kirkwall in the Orkneys.*

The Cathedral endures, but many buildings as striking in their way have withered or vanished down the centuries. The Castle is no more. The Bishop's Palace where Hakon died, a broken king after Largs, is a towered ruin. A ruin beautiful in spite of its dilapidation is the Earl's Palace nearby, exquisitely built by the architects of the seventeenth-century Stuart Earl of Orkney, Patrick: a Machiavellian creature, it seems, who had nevertheless a fine taste in the arts.

West front, St Magnus Cathedral, eight centuries old

It was about Patrick Stuart's time and afterwards, that Orkney had its great crop of witches – women old and young who, because of some physical malformation or quirk of character, drew parish gossip about themselves; or perhaps some of them did indulge in the ancient pre-Christian fertility rites that they thought necessary to keep the precarious wheel of agriculture fruitfully turning. Many of them met a wretched end – they had 'the red sark putten on them' – at the place called Gallowsha' (at the top of the steep road now called Clay Loan).

GALLOWSHA'

Three Old Women
'Bring in fire!' three old women cried. 'Give her the yellow and red coat!' . . . But no torches were lit before the throat was girdled.

Neighbour
Was as bonny a bairn as ever wore daisies, she. What worm comes in at the mouth when innocence sleeps? It breeds in the heart.

The Stranger
Oh yes, but she cried. She skirled when she saw the post and the rope! She stopped then. She went to the hangman laughing like to a bridegroom.

Preacher
Repent ye, therefore, and turn. Behold the tree of

The Kirk Loft, St Magnus:
'A hangman's ladder twa could clim
A widden pulpit, geen tae bits. . .'

A picture which once hung from
the 'Sailor's Loft' in the cathedral
(*Tankerness House Museum*)

sinners, that the rose petals thereof melt as snow, and are thorns and ashes soon.

Ale-wife
Ale, penny a pot. Cool the flame the poor girl stands in. Usque, twopence the glass. Warm a cold spirit. It passes.

A Palace Guard
He tried her this way and that, with smiles and sovereigns, then threatenings. She would not abide his cajolings under the moon. Then three strangers, with paper and seal, stood at her father's door.

Child
What's that black mask? What white thing is shaking under the rope? Mother, why seven torches, and the sun so bright?

Famous men – kings, writers, statesmen, warriors – have visited Kirkwall and gone again. One wonders what went through the mind of King James the Fifth as he stepped ashore from the little boat: only a few years before these islanders, confused in their loyalties, bereft of the protection of their ancient laws, resentful of the Scots who were lording it over them increasingly, had taken up arms and resoundingly beaten the royal army at Summerdale. King James brought unguents and salves: he revived the people's

St Magnus Cathedral,
begun 1137, completed
350 years later

St Magnus Cathedral,
north aisle of the nave

pride by giving Kirkwall royal burgh status (it was already a city by virtue of its cathedral).

Sir Walter Scott lingered in Kirkwall in 1814; for some reason he took a distaste to the town, and wrote an insulting little poem about it.

Tennyson and Gladstone arrived on a ship, Russia-bound. They were at once offered the Freedom of the City. Tennyson, wrapped in gloom, declined to speak at the ceremony, but the Prime Minister with his great rolling periods more than made up for that lack. The Poet Laureate left no lines about the city or the islands (one thinks that his interest might have been kindled a little by Orkney's place in the Arthurian cycle).

In a real sense Kirkwall has no need of imported fame: she has nurtured a wealth of scholars and artists. The poets Edwin Muir and Robert Rendall and Duncan J. Robertson went to school here, and Stanley Cursiter the Queen's Limner. About the turn of the century, Kirkwall Grammar School produced an astonishing crop of talent. Local boys and boys from the parishes and islands around passed on to one or other of the Scottish Universities, and after distinguished achievements there became professors in Britain and in almost every part of the empire. It is noteworthy perhaps that most of these brilliant men chose scientific disciplines: medicine, agriculture, botany, geology. Some people, like Dr Hugh Marwick, have argued that the Orcadian mind is practical rather than imaginative. The wealth of island culture from the beginning contradicts this; we should rather see the Orkney mind as an intermeshing of the practical

St Magnus Cathedral,
'the wonder and glory of the north'

and the imaginative, and this has been a constant pattern. The broch builders united supreme utility with a fine sense of form and structure. The Norsemen sailed to get Irish linen and girls, French wine-barrels, English silver, in ships of superb design. . . . Indeed, what is a poem or a carving on a stone? It was, originally, a spell to make the corn grow, to lure fish into the net; beauty and utility were one.

Nowadays, Kirkwall is a busy town. It seems all of Orkney is to be found there, on a Monday or a Saturday afternoon. Kirkwall continues to grow, while the parishes and islands are drained slowly of their populations. In the kind of centralising society that is the universal pattern nowadays, this imbalance is perhaps inevitable. But still many Orcadians wonder if it makes for the health of the total community.

A significant development of recent years has been the settling in Orkney of scores of families from the south, mainly England; they have come to rediscover old wholesome cycles of life that industrialism has been destroying for two centuries, and now with ever-increasing ruthlessness. But with oil flowing into Flotta from the North Sea, and an as-yet-untapped uranium belt in the Stromness–Sandwick area, no one can say how Orkney will look in the next half-century or so. Meantime, the great majority of the immigrants have settled down well with the Orcadians: within a generation, they should add a new rich strain to the already complex blood-strain of Orkney.

Visitors to Orkney must be surprised at the number of banks and building societies in Kirkwall especially. This is the modern equivalent of the ancient 'stocking under the bed'. The Orcadians have always been a prudent penny-wise people; which however has nothing to do with lack of generosity. On the farms especially, they cannot load enough food or drink on the table for guests or strangers.

On the outskirts of Kirkwall are two distilleries: Highland Park and Scapa. They both produce a uniquely flavoured malt whisky, that is becoming increasingly popular all over the world.

Supermarkets, banks, shops, hotels, busy piers and streets, the large web of government offices, housing schemes, hostels: Kirkwall is the busy heart of Orkney indeed. Inside the town there are places where you can escape the market-day bustle and rush: Tankerness House with its new marvellous little museum and, behind, a wide garden, rich in summer with blossom and bees, where you can sit and linger. Across the street, in the roseate gloom of St Magnus Cathedral, you step into history and the peace occasionally to be found at the heart of history. How did the interior of St Magnus look four and a half centuries ago, when one of our greatest bishops, Robert Reid (he founded Edinburgh University) reorganised the chapter? Some think that then, at the height of its glory, the cathedral was richly painted and ornamented, quite unlike the dim martyr-glow we move reverently through nowadays. Would there have been vivid Stations of the Cross along walls now studded with mournful seventeenth- and eighteenth-century tombstones? Between then and now, the Cathedral has suffered indignities – whitewash, Cromwell's horses, a storing of merchants' masts and spars. . . . Some people think St Magnus would be better now without the tombstones, and especially without the massive Victorian marble to Baikie and Rae, explorers. For all its immense hewn power, St Magnus should be seen too as a work of marvellous delicacy that can be spoiled by thoughtless tamperings.

Not so very long ago, on late summer evenings, the booths of the Lammas Market did their raucous flare-lit business in the shadow of the cathedral; until magistrates, fearful of irreverence, moved the coconut-men and cheap-jacks and fortune-tellers to a field in the outskirts. But all life – business, religion, fantasy – is a single weave, and we sunder it at our peril, perhaps. Of recent years, a St Magnus Fair has been initiated, and has already sent down roots; it too plies its tumultuous business just under the red walls of 'the old kirk', and all profits go to the maintenance of the cathedral itself – in recent years strains and cracks have been found in the fabric.

The midsummer St Magnus Festival of the arts, begun in 1977, is now firmly established in the Orkney calendar. Much of the music is performed inside the Cathedral. The main item of the opening festival was Peter Maxwell Davies' chamber opera *The Martyrdom of St Magnus*.

People come from all over Britain, and beyond, to attend the festival. The leading British journals and magazines give it generous space. Orkney, after long centuries, is once more a living centre of the arts.

The interior of Earl Patrick Stewart's
17th Century palace in Kirkwall

Rackwick, 'the bay
of wreckage', Hoy

Sea 4

Salt in the mouth,
The rage
Of north wind at morning,
Sodden crust,
Cold kissings of rain.
This unease
Is better than Ragna at her hearth.

Too late for rudder's turning
Back into history,
The old worn web,
King, lawman, merchant, serf.
The prow crashes
Into a new time.

They will say next winter
At the fire,
'Leif Ericson went
The fool's voyage.'
A man will sing to a harp
'Heroes
Do not venture only for bits of gold'.
An old woman will say
To girls at candle-time,
'It is that slut, the sea
Always
That has their hearts'.

'THE SWAN'S PATH', 'the whale road': with such kennings the Norsemen set out on the circling magnificence of the sea. What made them sail west from Norway was a complex thing: political and economic pressures, an insatiable curiosity, a lust for domination. They were marvellous seamen, venturing without compass in frail beautiful boats. They came to the snow and fires of Iceland. They even, for a time (until the climate worsened), wrung a livelihood from the bleakness of Greenland. Westwards still they went, and came on the painted feathered Indians and the wild grapes of North America, four centuries before Columbus.

Their longships had, long before, probed among the Shetlands and the Orkneys. The islands were inhabited by a dark sturdy imaginative people. The Vikings opened the place up with axe and fire, took what they wanted, and sailed off again. This must have happened time after time – a monotonous blood-splashed pattern. Yet they never forgot the fertility of the islands: fish, birds, corn. At last they came as settlers and farmers. What happened to the native Picts can only be imagined; at best they were enslaved and their women taken; the conquerors' story in the next few centuries is brilliantly told in *Orkneyinga Saga*.

In a cluster of islands like Orkney sea and land – stark opposites, irreconcilable – are inextricably mingled. They take richness and beauty from one another: the fish and the cornstalk, peatfire and fish-oil lamp, in one croft. The first Orcadians, whoever they were, tried to explain the mysterious unity of sea and land with a web of legend. The seals with their large eloquent

eyes and love of music are the link. They come ashore, cast their skins, dance on the sand in human form. A man, concealed in the long grass above, steals a pelt, and so the selkie lass cannot go back to her element; she is his, a croft-wife, till she dies or finds after many years her skin hidden in the barn rafters . . . or else a country girl sweet as milk is taken to Suleskerry or Hether–Blether the vanishing island by the seal-tribe, and never seen again.

The golden age of Orkney lasted three centuries or thereby: the great explorers, vikings, pilgrims were at last pearl and coral or kirkyard dust. The next few centuries certainly had its sailors, fishermen, beachcombers, but they have no names or stories. What emerges starkly is the people's ambivalent attitude to the sea. The sea was the great mother: she gave them, sometimes lavishly, sometimes stingily, from her stores of fish, whale, salt, tangle, driftwood. Winter after winter she hurled freighted ships on the rocks and crags; while the cargoes of rum or wheat or apples lasted, life in this island and that was a long winter festival. But the sea did not give for nothing; another of her names was 'the widow-maker'. From time to time the sea took a single life to herself, or at a stroke a whole ship's crew. And this was her due. Therefore, a man struggling in the sea need look for small help from those on shore; if he got to land, good and well; if he drowned, the sea was taking what was hers. In fact, it was dangerous and foolish to try to save a sea-embroiled man: the would-be rescuer was sure to suffer grievously for his presumption.

Orkney's first lighthouse, North Ronaldsay.
It dates from 1789.

This primitive double attitude to the sea, provider and destroyer, faded well over a century ago. The achievement of the Orkney lifeboats in the last hundred years is unequalled for resource and heroism. Tragedy in 1969 struck the Longhope lifeboat going to rescue a ship in difficulties: the entire crew was lost; within a few days a new crew of life-savers had volunteered.

The coast of Orkney is no longer a graveyard for ships. A scattering of lighthouses keeps benighted or storm-shaken ships on their safe sure ways.

There are hundreds of fascinating sea stories told in the islands: of smugglers, Armada survivors, King Hakon and Largs, the press-gang that terrorised Orkney crofts during the Napoleonic wars, the pirate Gow, the witches who sold good winds to skippers, merchants, fishermen, beachcombers, storm-watching women, whalers, Hudson's Bay traders, emigrants, Cook and Franklin who drew barrels of water at Logins Well in Stromness, the sinking of *Hampshire* and *Royal Oak*, the suicide in midsummer 1919 of the entire German Grand Fleet in Scapa Flow. A very moving story is of the death of a little Queen on shipboard on the North Sea.

The ship rode at anchor in the calm of a little voe.

The ship had limped out of the North Sea the day before, late: salt-encrusted, sail-torn.

Some of the islanders had come down to the shore, mostly women. The men were more cautious: they could see the foreign heraldry of Scotland on the stern. Strange ships meant, usually, trouble. The men waited round the crofts, ready to take to the hills.

But one man stood at the shore, slightly apart from the women. He was the farmer from The Bu, the chief man in the island.

From the shore they could see men on the ship, going about their business, but slowly, as if they were sailors in a gray sea dream. The sailors paid small attention to the island and the people on the shore.

A man in a gray cloak had stood since dawn at the helm: slowly he gestured here and there; slowly the sailors obeyed him. Needles were put into the torn sail. The salt scabs were scrubbed and washed from the handsome oak of the vessel.

Once the skipper at the helm turned his face shorewards. He raised his hand. The farmer, the laird, raised his hand in reply.

The women formed a circle then. They broke the long silence. Their faces were here and there. Their voices were sharp with inquisition.

The sun rose higher.

There was a dead child cradled in the ship, in a little oak-panelled cabin. Her hair was tangled like storm-beaten corn.

The dead girl lay on a narrow bed in the middle of the ship-chamber. She was clad in white linen. The sun came in at the cabin window and shone foursquare across her.

The cabin smelt still of spindrift and flung weed, but country airs too came in at the window now. All was in order, except that one of the lamps had been half-wrenched from its wall-bracket. It hung, twisted, just above the door.

The women in this death-room began to move. They moved even slower than the sailors outside on rigging and forecastle. It was as if they bent and turned to unheard harps.

One gathered the wild hair of the child and made a bright knot of it and tied it in a white ribbon. The other two took from a carved chest under the bed a long gown: it was blue satin, it was sewn about the bodice with hundreds of little pearls, it had silver clasps at shoulder and waist. After they had raised the small stiff body they sheathed it in that magnificent fabric. Then, once more, they crossed the thin hands one upon the other.

The dead child was as remote as a star: a first star in the new darkness of autumn, at harvest-time, that glitters magnificent and cold in a pool.

One of the women took a crystal phial from the sea-chest. She shook drops on to her long fingers. She touched, here and there, the face and broidered hair of the dead child.

The second woman smiled.

Late in the afternoon the skipper of the ship had himself rowed ashore in a small blue boat.

He walked up the beach to the farmer who stood, still, on the sea-bank above. The women hovered around, like gulls about a half-broken crust.

The skipper said to the laird: 'You are wondering no doubt what brings a strange ship into your bay. Sir, I ought to have informed you sooner. Other concerns prevented courtesy. We have come from Bergen in Norway. We are bound for Leith in Scotland. Between Norway and Scotland we ran into a storm, one of the worst I have experienced, and I am an old sailor. We carried the Queen of Scotland across the North Sea to her people and her throne. It was foreseen that some

Herring boat, Kirkwall

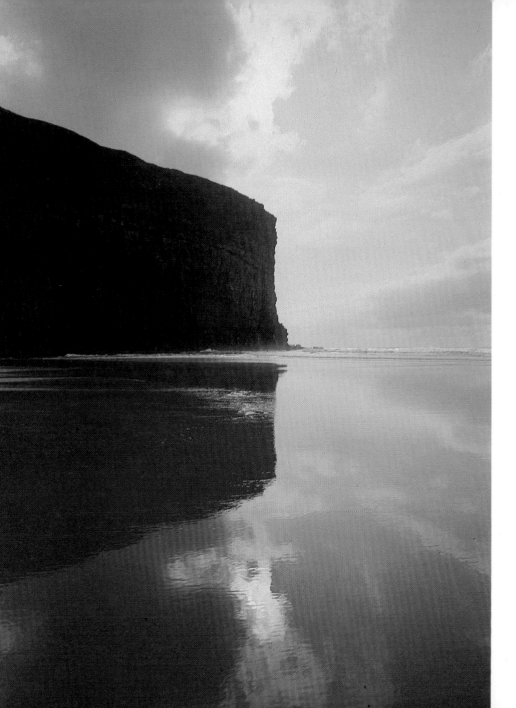

day she would be Margaret, Queen of Scotland and of England and of Norway also. Sir, she was a tender child of seven years, and the storm that made me gray in the face was the end of her.'

The laird shook his head in wonderment.

The women covered their heads. The wailing was spun from mouth to mouth: a thin gray web of grief.

That harbour, seven hundred years later, is called, still, St Margaret's Hope.

Now the islands are connected to each other, and to Scotland, by comfortable and efficient ferry-boats. The fishermen no longer sail alone to the creels in little yawls, for meagre uncertain returns. The modern fishing boats are bigger, well-manned, and relatively prosperous.

Occasionally, on the horizon, the islanders see the long silhouette of a tanker bound for Flotta and the oil tanks.

Units of the NATO fleet come and go in Scapa Flow, until recently the most famous anchorage in the hemisphere.

Only children nowadays take, seriously and wonderingly, the old legends of the seal-girl stolen to work in peatbank and furrow, of the croft girl sea-enchanted to selkie ways. There is one beautiful true story that sums up perhaps the hardships and charities of man in his dealings with the sea; it is one of the most moving episodes in *Orkneyinga Saga*. A Shetland crofter waits at the shore for his mate to come out fishing, in vain. It was

Rackwick

Oystercatchers near the
Hole o' Rowe, Skaill Bay

APRIL 1910

COALINC

SHIP.

Tombstone for a sailor lost at sea,
churchyard of St Magnus Cathedral

dangerous to fish alone, in the fierce off-shore tide. A man in a white hood – a stranger – hails him. He offers to row while the crofter-fisherman works the lines. The offer is accepted, but soon the poor fisherman wishes he had never seen the hooded man; for he rows at once into the fiercest whirls and tugs of the tide-stream, where the boat dances like a cork. (But there the best, strongest fish are to be found.) A basketful is perilously taken, then the oarsman rows with skill and power for the shore, where a group of women are waiting. The catch is divided. The cowled stranger gives his fish to the waiting women; then, as he turns away, he stumbles on a slippery stone, and the women laugh. The man picks himself up, replies with an impromptu poem on the harp of his mouth, the last line of which is, 'Who'd know that I was an earl? . . .' It is common knowledge before nightfall that the mysterious man is the great Earl Rognvald Kolson. The story encapsules the astonishing character of the man in all its facets: his humour, his daring, his charity, his gift for spontaneous poetry. It also illustrates what the sea means perennially to those who live beside it: danger, sudden bounty, trust, uncertainty, hunger. The crofter-fisherman, we presume, stayed at home with his plough and his few creels. Earl Rognvald was about to launch into the greatest venture of his life: the sea-pilgrimage to Jerusalem, Byzantium, Rome, in which piety and ancient Viking barbarism were so curiously mixed.

Stromness 5

THERE MUST always have been people living in or near Stromness. The inner end of the harbour was called Hamnavoe, 'the haven inside the bay'; so early fishermen knew it was a good place to keep their boats. The district to the north-east is called Cairston, a fertile stretch with fine farms on it, and, below, clusters of seals on the rocks. Indeed, the Castle of Cairston comes into *Orkneyinga Saga*; the people inside were besieged one Michaelmas; one man ran from the imminent storm of fire and axes all the way to Kirkwall, and didn't stop until his shield wedged in the wide door of the Cathedral.

The first recorded house was an inn at the very tip of the long blue tongue of sea that is the harbour, in 1580. The hosts were William and Mareon Clark. They had 'power of brewing and selling, keiping of ostelrie and bying of all thingis apperteining thairto for furnissing of the commounes and utheris resorting thairaway. . . .'

It is not likely that William Clark would open an inn for fishermen and farm folk, who lived on their own produce and refreshment. Large ships, many of them foreign, were beginning to drop anchor behind the two little sheep islands, the Holms, that form the eastern arm of the harbour. That entry in a lawyer's ledger is all we know about William and Mareon, the first recorded townsfolk. But the imagination delights to work on them.

Your door stood open wide
From the rising of the lark
To the pole of night, to all men,
    William and Mareon Clark.

You gathered about your fires
The crew of the wintered barque
From Lisbon, or Brest, or Boston,
    William and Mareon Clark.

Tired, you'd put out the lamps
Cover the fire, and hark!
A scatter of hooves on the cobbles.
    William and Mareon Clark. . . .

Nothing. You cannot hear us.
Two names, quilled and stark
On a lawyer's parchment, ghostings –
    William and Mareon Clark. . . .

Once a nucleus had formed, the little village (called variously then Hamnavoe, Cairston, Stromness) grew rapidly. It was not an easy place to build houses on. The granite hill called Brinkie's Brae slopes steeply from the west into the harbour. Out of the flank of Brinkie's Brae the new house foundations had to be hewn. On small stone piers protruding into the sea other houses were reared, gable-ended to the cold east and the winter sea-spray. One gets the impression that on a man's little enclosure or 'quoy' he crammed in as many houses as he could, to grow rich on

the rents. Yet the pattern of the town is beautiful, without (it seems) there being any overall plan in the minds of the merchants and landowners who threw it together so hurriedly and inconsiderately.

> *The street uncoiled like a sailor's rope from North to*
> *   South*
> *And closes swarmed up the side of the hill*
> *Among gardens and clouds,*
> *And closes stepped down to the shifting water*
> *And the nets and whitemaas. . . .*

The eighteenth century was Stromness's golden age. The recurring wars with France meant that much shipping sailed round the north of Britain, since the English Channel was unsafe. The shop-keepers grew wealthy on kroner, marks, doubloons, escudos: by this time Stromness was known all over Europe to be a safe anchorage from storms and privateers.

One young man about this time disgraced the name of Stromness. A local merchant, William Gow, had a son called John, who (like hundreds of his Orkney contemporaries) went to sea when he was still a lad. That was the last that was heard of him, until in the winter of 1725 an armed merchant-ship called *The George* anchored in Cairston Roads. The skipper stepped ashore, and he turned out to be John Gow. At once he was welcomed into the best local houses; he and the daughter of a local merchant fell in love, and exchanged pledges. The ordinary townsfolk, however, were disconcerted by the behaviour of

Stromness, once a great
port for Hudson's Bay ships
and whaling fleets   A Stromness street

Fishing boats at Stromness

Gow's crew, a patchwork of ruffians recruited (it seemed) from the sleaziest waterfronts of Britain. They fought, thieved, threatened, made rout and riot everywhere, molested the young women. By chance Gow's ship was recognised by a storm-bound skipper: she was really *The Revenge*, a pirate vessel that had been terrorising the North Atlantic all the preceding year. Gow, desperately attempting to escape the trap that was closing in, drove his ship against the Calf of Eday in the northern Orkneys; he was captured, tried, and executed in London with the worst of his shipmates in the summer of 1726. A dreadful story came to light as the trial unfolded: a mutiny in the Mediterranean on the ship *Caroline*, bound from Santa Cruz to Genoa: Captain Ferneau and all his officers murdered, except Ferneau's loved and trusted officer John Gow, to whom he had entrusted the key of the arms-chest.

As if to compensate for Gow, only a few years later history gave Stromness its hero, a merchant called Alexander Graham. In those days the merchants of all small ports in Scotland had to pay cess-money to the royal burghs before they could engage in trade. So Stromness was in thrall, to this extent, to Kirkwall. Graham, with great skill and determination, organised his fellow-merchants to refuse payment of the cess. Court action after court action ended, many years later, in the House of Lords: a victory for Stromness and Graham, but not only for them, for all the many Scottish ports similarly bled by the royal burghs. A few years later Graham died in poverty; he had ruined himself with legal costs. There is not even a gravestone to him in the kirkyard.

Carrick House, Eday.
Here Gow the pirate
was lured and taken
by the laird, James Fen,
in 1725.

There was an old hag of nearly a hundred who lived in a hovel on the side of Brinkie's Brae when a lawyer and poet and lighthouse commissioner called Walter Scott came to Orkney on the lighthouse ship *Pharos* in 1814. His poetry, though popular and romantic, did not pay. Now he was on the lookout for plots for novels. He was told that Bessie Millie, the old storm-brewer, remembered John Gow well. She told him enough to set his imagination working: a few years later the fruits of the seed sown that day in Stromness appeared, a novel called *The Pirate*, in which the poor old Stromness witch who sold favourable winds to sailors at sixpence a time became the towering sibyl Norna of Fitful Head.

Pirate and hero and witch flourished in the eighteenth century. The next century is empty of names, but Stromness continued to grow and prosper. Ships of the Hudson's Bay Company called at Stromness for a last provisioning, and also to take to the trading posts of Canada young Orkneymen who had otherwise little outlet for their energies in the overcrowded crofts of home. They turned out to be good workers. Many of them made substantial fortunes in 'the nor-west'. Many never saw Orkney again; but such surnames as Flett, Foubister, Folster, linger still among the Canadian Indians. . . . Whalers too called at Stromness to complete their crews; their wages, when they got home from the Davis Straits about harvest time, were welcome in the hand-to-mouth crofts. . . . There were one or two boom years in Stromness, also, when vast herring harvests were landed. But the sea, as always, gave her treasures capriciously. Lean and

For emigrants, voyagers, merchants: notice of sailing (*Tankerness House Museum*)

The pier at Stromness: cargo-boats, fishing boats

hungry seasons followed the years of the endless silver torrents, and at last this uncertain traffic came to an end.

Across the bay from Stromness is the Hall of Clestrain. In that big house was born the Orkney explorer Dr John Rae. When the two ships *Erebus* and *Terror*, in the mid-nineteenth century seeking for the elusive 'north-west passage' vanished, the whole nation quickened with interest and speculation. (It was the great age of mapping the blank areas of the globe.) What had happened to the famous navigator Sir John Franklin? It was Rae and his Orkneymen who discovered the truth, from the mouth of an Eskimo. The thick short fish-smelling smiling one produced, as evidence, forks and coins and sashes taken from the ice-doomed sailors. The two great ships had been crushed like matchwood in the bergs and floes. (Incidentally, Stromness had been the last port and watering-place of the Franklin expedition.)

'In the ice village, no information.
We must first sit at a fish-board
Lit with smiles. . . .
'In the House of Ice (he said)
Iron and oak are frail flowers, bone
Is subtle and lasting.
Our creatures came kindly about the strangers.
Birds, fish offered help.
They could not understand. The greeting
Withered in the air.
They could not reply, laughing,
Come, caribou. Come, wolf. Come, snow-bird.
They were ghosts before death
One after another, drifting
In bright and dark circles, untrysted.
We watched, just under the horizon'. . . .

James Watt, when he watched his mother's kettle boiling, foreshadowed (among many marvels of the Industrial Age) the decline of Stromness. The ugly steam ships when they came had not such need as the old beautiful sailing ships of shelter and provisioning. Gradually the pulse of the town slowed down. The population dwindled. The boat-building yards and the coopers' yards fell silent. Herring stations were abandoned. The distillery that produced the famous 'Old Orkney' malt whisky closed its doors. The period between the two world wars was the bleakest time in Stromness's history. Young people who grew up then had a sense of decline and stagnation. Even the public houses, fifty years before so numerous along the street, had had to put up their shutters.

The outlook is much brighter now. There is boat-building again, bigger fishing craft in the west and a better market for the fish, toffee-making, a thriving tourist industry; a sense of stir and purpose everywhere.

What can never be taken away from the town is a unique beauty. The stone web will always be there between Brinkie's Brae and the sea. The single surging twisting street is admired by all visitors to Stromness. But what they too seldom visit are the closes that swarm up the side of the hill, and the steps that seek down to the twenty creeled and salty piers, washed twice a day by cold incoming Atlantic waters.

Behind Stromness: 'a tumult of roofs'

6 Stone

'THE ISLANDS OF STONE' they could have been called: there is so much of it everywhere, little fissures in the earth and immense quarries have yielded stone from the time of the first settlement five or six thousand years ago. Men, generation by generation, have turned the stone into things beautiful and useful, grand and simple and good.

They had to use stone. The salty Atlantic winds have seen to it that no trees flourish, except in little sheltered folds of the hills.

Stone served for the living and the dead. The first Orkney folk must have seen life as a brief flickering flame; few of them lived to be thirty years old, and most of them were probably crippled with rheumatism and respiratory troubles (the same salty dampness that rusts cars nowadays is, at all times, hard on flesh and bone). Death must have seemed to those early fowlers and limpet-gatherers the dark enduring reality: the opposite and complement of their few summers and winters. So to death were reared the best houses: Maeshowe in Stenness is a magnificent burial chamber, the stones of the long entrance corridor so placed that the last light of midwinter enters and splashes briefly one of the tombs: a seed of light sown in the womb of night, winter, death.

A few fields away from Maeshowe are the 'standing stones' that give the parish of Stenness its name. It might never be known what exactly these monoliths are for – astronomy, religion, sacrifice, fertility – argument and speculation have been shuttled back and fore since men decided to dispense with legend; and still we are no nearer the truth. Mediaeval Orcadians, before the days of reading and counting, wanted to know what the stones were, too. They came to a communal conclusion; they were giants that had been suddenly petrified. Creatures of darkness, the giants had to be home and quarry-fast before the sun got up: otherwise it would go ill with them. Possibly there was some kind of giants' feast at Stenness, between the two lochs, one summer night. Faster and faster the bucket of mead went from mouth to mouth; the bones of mammoth and whale were crunched. A few of the more cautious giants, seeing the first flush in the north-east, thought it was time to be getting off home; and they left the party, singly or in groups. The reckless ones, flushed with drink and fellowship, circled round in yet another moor-dance. Wind piped between the hills – wind stroked the dark glimmering strings of the loch; to that primitive music the reel went round. The sun suddenly looked at them from between two clouds, and that was the end of the Orkney giants. All were turned to stone, even the prudent ones hurrying home to the quarry at Vestrafiold.

The little neolithic stone village of Skara Brae on the west coast of Orkney is a place that touches the heart, because it is on such a human scale: giants and trolls have no place in it; it is a cluster of houses where we can see that people moved and lived and loved; their simple stone artefacts lie everywhere around – dressers, beds, doorposts. A sudden sandstorm, it's said, ended its brief anonymous history. Another westerly gale, thousands of years later, swept the sand blanket away: nineteenth-century laird and crofter and fisherman looked down, awed, at the abode of their

remote ancestors, herdsmen and fishermen:

> *As I came home from Sandwick*
> *A star was in the sky.*
> *The northern lights above the hill*
> *Were streaming broad and high.*
> *The tinkers lit their glimmering fires,*
> *Their tents were pitched close by.*
> *But the city of the vanished race*
> *Lay dark and silent in that place.*
> *As I came home from Sandwick*
> *A star was in the sky.*

In a sense we have never fully shrugged off the Stone Age. Within living memory people were sleeping in stone beds. The great millstones that gave the people their bread and ale have, only lately, lost their fruitful thunders. In spite of concrete and imported wood, the best new houses are still built of local stone; they come out of the quarries strong and beautifully-hued. Stromness will always, to the end of its days, be a stone town like Skara Brae: its score of piers stone feet in the ebb.

A cottage in Rackwick, Hoy   House interiors of Skara Brae

Overleaf

The Dwarfie Stone, Hoy:
bronze age tomb or anchorite's dwelling?

The Dwarfie Stone, interior

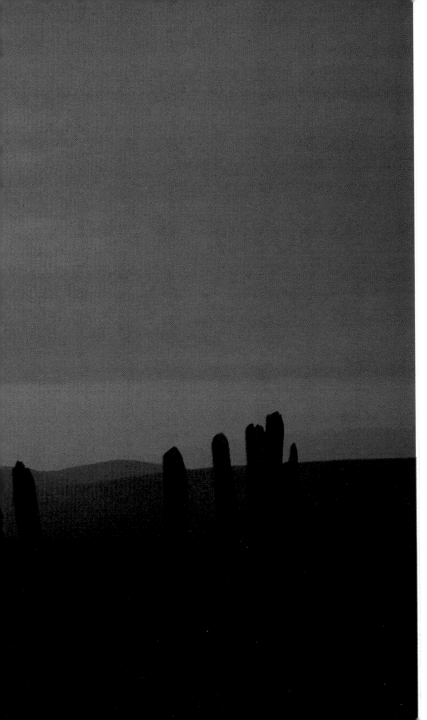

It's said that St Magnus once wished to cross the Pentland Firth. There was no boat or boatman handy. He launched a stone from the Caithness shore, and standing on it came safe to Orkney. At a church in South Ronaldsay is the very stone with the saint's foot-marks on it.

But, to pass from mediaeval miracle, men have written their hearts on the native stone. As remarkable as the stone symbolism of life and death and rebirth in Maeshowe are the runes cut by Norse crusaders on those same walls in the winter of 1151. The fifteen ships sheltered and provisioned in Scapa before taking the sea-road to Narbonne, Jerusalem, Micklegarth, Rome: some of the Viking pilgrims dug their way into the mysterious howe, either out of lust for gold or to prove their courage. On the walls they cut graffiti: INGIBIORG IS THE LOVELIEST OF THE GIRLS and MANY A PROUD WOMAN HAS HAD TO ENTER HERE LOW STOOPING and JERUSALEM-FARERS BROKE IN HERE and HERMUND OF THE HARD AXE CARVED THESE RUNES, and many more; besides cuttings of dragon and walrus.

This writing on stone still goes on, of course. It is a moving experience to wander through any seaside Orkney kirkyard and read the brief biographies of the vanished dead. To wander, and linger, and read, is still to arouse fragrant ghosts.

Always, by the shore, kirk and kirkyard.
Legends of men, their carved names
Faced east, into first light, among sea sounds.

The gravestones are placed to take the risen sun.

The Ring of Brodgar. 27 of the original 60 monoliths in this great monument of the early bronze age still stand. The circle is over a hundred yards in diameter.

So stone fought, over the centuries, its stubborn wars against the new materials: bronze Pictish axes, the silver and gold coins of merchants, iron of plough and clinkered gate and ship, the cans and kettles of wandering tinkers, steel hulls of battleships sunk under Scapa Flow and Marwick Head.

> *The stranger waded ashore.*
> *His axe-blade*
> *Bright as the sun, rang once on a stone.*
> *Then all the stone axes*
> *Withered in an hour. Then runes*
> *Were dumb before harp and high voice.*

Indeed the metals, when first they came, were looked on as magical materials. An iron stake in the lintel of a house kept trows and evil spirits out. The holy island, Eynhallow, was plucked out of timelessness by another iron spell. It is not (at the time of writing) certain that uranium is to cast the same enchantment over twentieth-century Orcadians.

Yet stone, the first and the humblest material, has yielded here memorable and beautiful things. Did the planners of St Magnus Cathedral think, while the dream grew in them, of those vast sandstone cliffs that stretch all the way from Westray to Hoy? Did they decide to draw on that awesome strength for their church, so that it would be 'the wonder and glory of all the north'? They knew for sure that sanctity is not all meekness.

Hoy cliffs

Yesnaby, Orkney's West Coast

Inside the chambered cairn
of Maeshowe (*c.* 1500 BC):
place of tombs and runes

Religion 7

WE DON'T KNOW what gods or nature spirits the first Orcadians held in awe and veneration. The seasons turned. In spring the grass came up, the birds returned north, lambs and calves were born. Summer was a good time, brimming with light and fertility. Then came the bronze and russet of autumn. They must have watched the onset of winter with dread. The wick of the sun, so high and potent in summer, was turned lower and weaker. The rain was no longer a filler of springs and a fosterer of grass and herbs; it had a hostile icy edge to it. . . . It was likely indeed that time would resume its cycles, and the seed would be waiting under the snow for its vernal summons. But there was no certainty about it: the exquisite equilibrium of the seasons might fail, overbalance from the strong centre. Then the sun would be a cold stone in the sky, and the whole of living things be sheathed in endless frost: grass and well and the lips of young lovers.

The circle of stones at Brodgar: is it a sun symbol? So long as men made appropriate sacrifices there, there would always be a time to love and a time to be born and a time to die for all things – crops and beasts and men. The balance would hold; the slow year-long pulse of the sun in the sky would not desert its treaty with men, symbolised by the circle on the moor. (A circle has no end or beginning.) And yet the moor was dark and barren, a patch of winter between the two lochs. There are minglings of image and of subtle metaphysical dialectic at which we can only dimly guess.

There is no mistaking the midwinter splash of light on the great house of death, Maeshowe. Here the symbolism is daring and triumphant. The torch is plucked from the dying hands of the year: a new time has begun.

The men of Brodgar and Maeshowe were, as well as builders, seekers into the hidden nature of things.

Circle of light and darkness, be our sign,
We move in shadows.
Brodgar has set on the moor a dance of sun.

Ring of quern and plough, contain
Our tumults of blood.
The stars' chaos is caught in a strict rein.

Wheel of winter and frost, remove
The sweet warm breath.
Ingibiorg flowers in stone, all beauty and love.

All religions, possibly, have their origin in this universal cycle of death, renewal, fulfilment, waning. Nowhere is the drama of light and darkness enacted with such starkness as in the north.

The priest-kings and worshippers of the early Orkney tribes vanished. The Norsemen who first plundered and then settled had their own pantheon: of whom the most appealing by far is Balder the Beautiful, the god of light. Word came at last of a doom upon Balder: he must die soon. But who or what would want to do an injury to this darling of the gods? His mother set out on a painful journey through the earth. She wrung promises from every living thing, plant and animal and bird, earth and sea and sky, that they would never hurt Balder. At last, her mission

accomplished, she turned her steps homeward. True, there was one plant at the wintry edge of the world, far far away, called mistletoe, that she hadn't bothered to visit. It was a pale sickly growth – inconceivable that it could ever harm the radiant immortal body of Balder.... But Loki, the mischief-maker, contrived one day of high sport in Asgard to put a spear made of mistletoe into the hand of a blind god. All the gods, to reassure Balder that he was invulnerable and immortal, had set him in the centre of a ring and were deluging his brightness with all kinds of missile. The blind god, in order to do honour to the one they all loved so much, flung the mistletoe; it pierced Balder's heart, and he died.

But Balder returns each spring, and the days of darkness and mistletoe and ice are forgotten. A green wave goes over the world, again and again.

The plot is the same; only the masks and the scenes are different. We may be sure the Picts, and the tribes before them, had their own forgotten stories to explain winter and summer, death and harvest, light and darkness.

It is but one step from those deeply ingrained beliefs to the knowledge of good and evil. Man perhaps becomes increasingly aware of himself as an individual: the tides of light and darkness mesh in his own heart; that is all eventually that need concern him, what D. H. Lawrence called disparagingly 'the isolate salvation of the single soul'. Yet to ignore the unity of the tribe, the nation, the race, is to go against the grain of the human spirit from the beginning. We are all indissolubly involved in each

Midhowe stalled cairn, Rousay:
a stone age burial chamber

other and in the whole totality of human kind, dead and unborn, from the beginning to an unforeseeable end. 'No man is an island.'

The first Christians were there already, Celtic monks and missionaries: they went with mild mouths and dove-shaped hands among the doom-ridden Norsemen of Orkney; and no doubt many a monk who had been spirit-kindled by Columba and Ninian in the west had their martyrdom sealed by axe and fire.

Time passed; Orkney was converted to Christianity in a singular yet typical fashion. Earl Sigurd, on shipboard at Osmundwall off the island of Hoy, had an unexpected sea visit from his liege-lord King Olaf of Norway. The king said, 'Either you consent to be baptised now, or every man of you will be killed.' So Sigurd and his men became reluctant Christians there and then. To see that there would be no backsliding, King Olaf took Earl Sigurd's son, a boy called Hundi, back with him to Norway. Hundi died there in a short time. Sigurd reverted to the gods of his fathers; he died fighting against the Christian High King of Ireland, Brian Boru, at Clontarf in Ireland.

In spite of Earl Sigurd's relapse, Christianity had taken root, and it spread rapidly. It was a great-grandson of the same fate-ridden Sigurd who gave the most extreme and dramatic witness to Christianity in the north.

On Easter Monday, 1117, two men confronted each other in the island of Egilsay: Hakon Paulson and Magnus Erlendson. These men, cousins, were joint earls of Orkney. Double rule, or even treble rule, had been a commonplace in the history of the earldom. It suited the purposes of the king of Norway, the overlord; a divided earldom was never in danger of asserting itself as a strong semi-independent entity. But the consequences, generation after generation, for the commons of Orkney were woeful and bitter: taxmen everywhere, soldiers in the corn-fields, a burning of mill and homestead.

Hakon and Magnus had come together to heal the always-opening wound. It was to have been a peace-meeting. Magnus

came, the dove in his hand. Hakon came with a gang of armed ruffians. An execution was carried out: Lifolf, Earl Hakon's cook, drove the axe into Magnus's forehead, weeping as he did so.

And that was that. With a single stroke Hakon had united the earldom. Politically it had been a wise – indeed the *only* – thing to do. Earl Hakon proved himself afterwards to be an able, strong, and generous governor, 'so that (the *Saga* says) the Orkneymen desired to have no other earl but him. . . .'

But strange things were happening in secret northern places. People with harelips and black coughs and scabs and deranged minds and quenched eyes began to go, or to be led, to the murdered earl's tomb in Birsay. They crossed the ebb to the steep green island where the church was, carrying their candles and offerings, and many of them were cured. The cult of Magnus spread rapidly all over the north; the common people canonised the slain earl years before the church called him Magnus Martyr.

Now the bones – cleft skull and all – lie in a pillar of the red Cathedral in Kirkwall that bears his name.

The man who ordered the building of St Magnus Cathedral was Magnus's nephew, Earl Rognvald Kolson, one of the most attractive figures in *Orkneyinga Saga*. Besides the great minster at the heart of Orkney, Earl Rognvald ordered the building of a fine ship in Norway, gold inlaid, with benches for seventy rowers. This was to be the principal ship of a fleet of fifteen, bound on a pilgrimage to Jerusalem: a holy voyage. With Earl Rognvald sailed the Bishop of Orkney, William the Old, and many of the finest young men from Scandinavia and the islands. It turned out

'Some frail memorial. . .'
a cathedral carving

St Magnus Church, Egilsay:
the island of the Saint

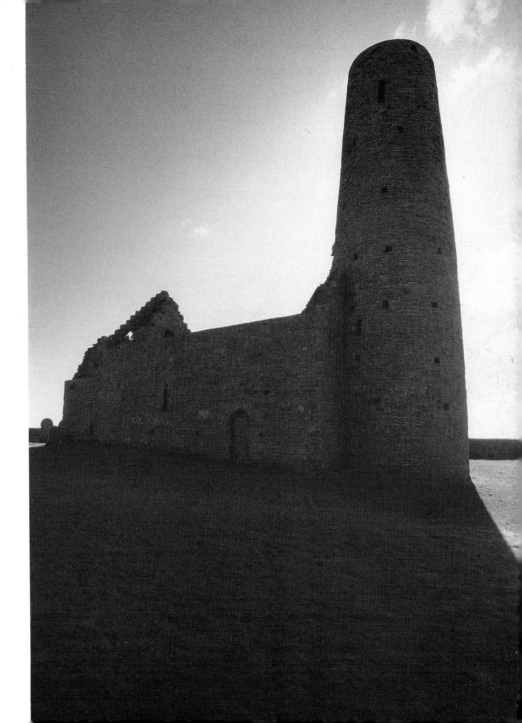

to be no voyage of unsullied piety: they mingled with their eternal yearnings such immediate necessities as war, love, and piracy. But in the end, bearing palm branches, they stood among the bright stones of Jerusalem.

After his brutal death in Caithness Rognvald – scholar, pilgrim, chess-player, poet – was called saint also.

Orcadians have never been zealots in religion. The Reformation, when it came in the mid-sixteenth century, seems to have been a quiet affair, carried out in some council chamber rather than in the burning hearts of men. At any rate, the Cathedral survived the change. Two centuries later, Orkney peasants were still leaving votive offerings in the ruins of the old chapels that were everywhere in the islands: occasion of many a thunderous sermon from eighteenth-century pulpits.

Many of those Presbyterian ministers were extraordinary men: classicists like Rev William Clouston of Stromness, naturalists like Rev George Low of Birsay and Dr Charles Clouston of Sandwick, eccentrics like Rev John Gerard of South Ronaldsay (he was a man of massive common sense and humour, but with a streak of melancholy).

In the nineteenth century Orkney must have been black with ministers; secession after secession from the established Church of Scotland meant that some parishes and islands had as many as three ministers at one time. Nowadays the number of clergymen is much what it was two centuries ago: ecumenism is all, these days.

There is one building in a little uninhabited island that tourists flock to by the thousand each summer. Italian prisoners of war helped with the construction of the huge Churchill barriers that link five islands together across the vulnerable east side of Scapa Flow. The Italian soldiers stayed on a bleak islet called Lamb Holm. Nothing on earth could have been more different from the vales of Tuscany and the little mediaeval towns of home, with winepress, olives, and bell-tower. Perhaps as much out of homesickness as of religious impulse they began to build, from two nissen huts and any scrap of metal and wood they could lay hands on, a little church; and they painted and decorated it inside in the Mediterranean tradition. (Earl Rognvald and his pilgrims would have known at once what the Italian soldiers were doing.) For a time after the war the little chapel was threatened with rot and rust. In the end it was saved by local people who saw that this was a beautiful place, and also perhaps a symbol of reconciliation and peace. The chapel was restored by one of the original builders, Domenico Chiochetti. Now, once a month each summer, a mass is said there.

A lonely grave between two parishes, Hoy and Walls: Betty Corrigall, suicide, buried in unconsecrated ground

Burray and the gas flare at
the installation of the Occidental
North Sea Consortium on Flotta

Occupations 8

THAT HUGE gas flare at the centre of Scapa Flow, the blazon that illumines Orkney's night sky, might well stand as a sign of the new industrial age, 'things to come'. Between the oil wells under the North Sea and the tanks of Flotta stretch, unseen, the vast veins and arteries of the new technology. Tankers bigger than some of the islands come and go between Scapa Flow and the refineries and oil-hungry nations near and remote.

The Orcadians take it with a strange casualness, as if nothing on earth or undersea really surprised them. They have, of course, been conditioned for three generations or so; ever since, on a late summer night in 1914, the people of Hoy saw the battleships of Britain steaming silently into Scapa Flow. . . . The pulse has never really been silent since. A major industry between the wars was the salvaging of the self-sunk German Fleet from those same gray depths. That work was still going on when World War Two broke out. At once Orkney was invaded by regiments and battalions and squadrons of soldiers and airmen. The navy returned, anxiously; for now Scapa Flow was well within the radius of air attack, and, as it proved, of deadly submarine attack – the war was only a few weeks old when Prien's torpedoes sank the *Royal Oak*.

Ruins of army encampments lie everywhere – fighter aerodromes in the centre of the fertile West Mainland – naval piers and concealed storage tanks in the island of Hoy: Orkney has been inured to huge influxes of men and money, and to the shapes of the machine age. The ugly concrete scars of 1939–45 still disfigure our countryside here and there. What could be more incongruous than the magnificent coastline of Yesnaby scabbed with the remnants of a naval gunnery range? The trouble with modern building materials is that time sours and stains them; whereas the local stone used for six thousand years and more weathers to beauty and aptness, as if buildings and landscape were made for each other.

Compared to the convulsion of 1914 and 1939, the oil industry is a smallish affair, that seems unlikely, in the long run, to make a large dent on the history and ecology of the islands.

What Orcadians fear – though they rarely speak about it – is that there might well be an accidental oil spillage that would pollute our coast lines from North Ronaldsay to Stroma. The local fishermen, of course, fear for their livelihood. But conservationists and those concerned with the natural environment – Orkney has plenty of such guardians – are keeping vigilant eyes on the situation.

'Things to come' may appear in more ominous disguises. It is known that there are deposits of uranium ore in Orkney, especially in a thick belt stretching from the north end of Stromness to Yesnaby. Recently the South of Scotland Electricity Board asked for permission to do some test borings. The move provoked immediate and spontaneous outcry. Petitions of protest were starred with thousands of signatures; the BBC and ITV sent up reporters and television teams; there was a solemn winter morning march along the streets of Kirkwall, in which Orcadians of all ages took part, to hand in the petitions at the offices of the Islands Council.

This popular protest was strange in a way, coming from a people that dislikes demonstration and outward flourishes. In one mood, indeed, the Orcadians seem to be oversold on the idea of progress and the exploitation of their own natural resources. They have never been averse to the idea of surpluses of money spilling over into the local economy.... The recent world-wounds of Hiroshima and Nagasaki are still vivid in the memory; and even the peaceful use of uranium seems to them fraught with dangers unknown before to humanity, that look as if they might take decades or centuries to resolve. . . . In addition, Orcadians have come to have a deep love of the physical appearance of their islands; the thought of possible open-cast mining in a lovely region of Orkney deeply disturbs them. The Geiger counter, pulsing madly near Cairston Mill – it was shown on our TV screens – might have excited Orcadians in other circumstances; it seemed an ominous symbol in the winter of 1977.

There is another side to the uranium issue, which physicists and geologists and politicians will argue. But a people's deep instinctive urges ought never to be discounted. The land is theirs, after all, and the earth-wisdom that comes from many generations of work on it.

From the beginning of June until the end of September, each year in increasing numbers, Orkney is thronged with tourists. They come by air and sea; cars by the thousand are ferried across the Pentland Firth on the drive-on M.V. *St Ola*. Orkney in high summer is like a shaken ant-hill. What is intriguing is that, unlike ants, our summer-time tourists have an almost infinite variety. In the 1930s, the tourists seemed to consist mainly of elderly genteel people, and a few eccentrics. Ladies would set up easels before Melvin Place or Flaws' pier in Stromness and discreetly apply water-colour splashes; gentlemen would roam the hillsides with binoculars and bird-books. The nature-lovers still come, amateur archaeologists, those in search of unspoilt sources; and there is, on the whole, adequate hotel and bed-and-breakfast accommodation for them. But, increasingly, it is the younger tourists who swarm in, from all over Europe and beyond; they live, for the most part, in hostels and tents; and they stir some freshness, adventure, excitement into our quiet round. The Orcadians, being a curious and friendly people, get on well with those gay invaders; who, apart from all else, deposit each year another thin layer of gold on the island economy.

The inherent wealth of the soil goes into the famous products of two distilleries in Kirkwall – Highland Park and Scapa. Their malt whiskies are becoming increasingly popular everywhere; and their rare tinctures enrich other famous blended whiskies.

Two creameries, in Kirkwall and Birsay, produce the popular 'Claymore' butter and cheese, and 'Swannay' cheese. In this farm and that, of course, the keeper of the hearth still makes her own distinctive cheese, butter, bannocks, ale, jam.

Boat-building has of course been an island craft for many generations. Duncans' yard in Burray; Scarths' and Sinclairs' in Stromness, Halmatic in Kirkwall, produce fine craft that are exported all over the world.

North Ronaldsay Mill, beside the remains of an earlier windmill

Overleaf

The Click Mill, Dounby: a rare example of a corn watermill, driven by a horizontal mill wheel

The Click Mill, interior

Thirled to boat-building is the oldest industry of all – fishing – the hunt through the sea for the gray and silver legions; nets let down for the armoured ocean-bed samurai – lobster and crab. Fishing has always been a precarious occupation, and always will be. Hardly a year passes without young men being lost somewhere along the Orkney coast.

> *Houses went blind*
> *Up one steep close, for a*
> *Grief by the shrouded nets.*

Besides the danger of his trade, the fisherman of only a generation ago was poorly rewarded. In the 1920s the inshore fishermen, working the lines from small boats, afterwards would sell their haddocks at threepence a pound from hand-barrows along the streets of Stromness.

Since the setting-up of the Orkney Fishermen's Society the whole outlook has changed in the fishermen's favour: live lobster, frozen crab and scallop, have found eager markets as far away as London, Paris, Amsterdam, Copenhagen. At present there are crab processing factories in Stromness, Westray, Rousay. The fishing future is brighter than it has ever been; except in the great nineteenth-century herring harvests that dazzled and over-whelmed and left at last a great desolation behind.

In Stromness there is a prosperous toffee factory – Robertson's Orkney fudge, like Highland Park whisky, and live lobsters out of Hoy Sound, is enjoyed all over the world.

Beautifully designed jewellery, with local motifs, is created in

The weapons of the whale-men,
from the Kirkwall whaler *Ellen*
(*Stromness Museum*)

two separate workshops in Kirkwall. There are (of course) knitwear firms. Potteries have recently been set up in country districts, and the products are full of imagination and fine craft: a home-brew set, consisting of a jug and half dozen mugs, seen recently in Tormiston Mill, had the true Orkney countryside grained into it.

New ventures burgeon everywhere, in unlikely places. The island of Sanday even has a small successful electronics firm, that makes and exports language laboratories, among other things.

So, modern Orkney is a pattern of industries old and new; and no one can say what the kaleidoscope will show at the next shaking.

Whatever the future holds, it seems likely that the last Orcadians, like the first, will be a pastoral agricultural fishing people. Without the earth-worker – who has often been despised in the past by ignorant urban people on account of the 'dust and dung' he has to work among – without the farmer, no civilisation past or future is conceivable. Behind symphonies, great art and literature, politics and philosophy and law, is the cornstalk.

Nowadays agriculture in Orkney is highly mechanised; it was a curious phenomenon, a century ago, that Orcadians took to the machine so fervently – almost as if they had been waiting for its advent patiently for a long time. 'How things work' has always fascinated the Orkneyman. Toil on croft and farm, in the early nineteenth century and before, must have been hard and anxious and arduous. . . . Yet it is a moving experience to wander round a place of ruined crofts, like Rackwick in Hoy, and see the ploughs

Log-board, used on whaling ships
(*Stromness Museum*)

slowly rusting at gable-end, and the quernstones that ground the people's oats set up against the wall as ornaments; and the kiln at Crowsnest a slow dilapidation.

There was an order and ceremony there that is lost forever.

To look much further back, to the very beginning. The first Orkneymen only fished perhaps in the rock pools for limpet, whelk, mussel. In a lucky time, a whale might blunder ashore. We may imagine a time when there was famine even in the ebb. It is in such seasons of peril that, suddenly, a single imagination is quickened. A young man, anxious and hungry, scratched on stone the curve of a boat, the curve of an oar, the curve of a sail: next winter the doors of Skara Brae were hung with Atlantic fish. . . . Image begets image. Perhaps it was not so long after, that a herdsman of the people, watching his sheep at their grazing, said, wonderingly, 'Why shouldn't the earth give nourishment to men as well as to beasts?' The answer to that question were the curves of plough, sickle, quern.

So the crofter-fisherman came with his signs; and his coming transformed society beyond recognition.

Whatever 'things to come' happen, may a saving imagination never fail us.

The wheel between flock and wintered folk
(*Tankerness House Museum*)

Broch of Gurness, Evie. Brochs were probably early Celtic 'keeps', their round towers rising to about 80 feet.

War 9

ELSEWHERE in this book, mention has been made of Orkney's 'golden age' – the time of the Norse earls, with their great hospitable halls and their beautiful ships and their retinues of poets. But even the best of times – the last years of Earl Thorfinn and the wise firm rule of Earl Hakon the saint-killer – were threatened with violence from beyond the horizon and laced red with private feud and murder. The only golden age for the peasant and his family was a year when the corn came up thick and burnished for the sickles of peace. The peasant knew, more vividly than those in power, how precarious life is: the armed horseman rides through his green corn, he is likely to be dragged from his hearth if the island chief is short of an oarsman for his spring pirate-voyage.

Raid, siege, battle go, a fatal undersong, through the history of the islands. Here and there, along sea coast or at loch-side are the remnants of brochs. These are marvellously-constructed primitive keeps or castles, and almost impregnable. The two concentric walls of a broch are bound together by a stone circling stair inside; any besieger rash enough to sit outside would be instantly and incessantly deluged with stone, arrow, fire, ordure. Any besieger hoping to starve the garrison into surrender needed long patience: for inside the broch would be food enough to last for as long as was necessary, and, at the centre, a well of ever-brimming water. The heart of the besieger might well quail, looking day after day (from a respectable distance) at the solid blank dangerous stone beehive.

But the broch builders themselves must have put the yoke on an earlier people: it has been suggested that the idea of trows came from those conquered original folk whom they drove into the interior hills and marshes, but who ventured out by night with noose and knife to take vengeance on the Celtic usurpers. Nobody knows how many waves of conquest went over the islands from the time of the first settlers. Certainly much that was rare and beautiful must have been destroyed in those anonymous centuries.

The Norsemen are still looked on as the greatest and most colourful in all the long procession of islanders, from stone-age men to Scots, and indeed they had many admirable qualities: stoicism, humour, resource, a rough-and-ready code of law, a taste for narrative, a fine contempt of death. But they in their turn destroyed what must have been a well-integrated artistic society.

The first ones came. They had no wings on their helmets. They were gaunt and sea-gray. They offered bits of bronze. The people of the island gave them bread and milk. They turned their lean ship round.

The next ones, twenty years later, came with hides, silver and walrus ivory. An axe glinted here and there. They asked if there was land for sale. One of the sailors pointed to a dark girl.

They dribbled in, over a decade: by shipwreck or design or exile. Islanders set a shivering one before the peat-fire.

They came at last in a huge bronze wave. They had nothing to trade. They possessed the wells, the barns, the glebes. They made songs in praise of wolf and hawk. They herded together the girls with black hair.

These are our heroes, the lauded ones. Praise rather the first breakers of the earth, the hewers of stones, the subtle ones who divined water and opened wells. It is their quiet voices that will end the story.

The Norse centuries in Orkney were stimulating as flung spindrift, but that time can also be looked at in another way. An Icelandic poet saw the marvellous tapestry as a web of ghastliness and insane rage, into which the hearts and entrails of the great warriors were gathered.

The warp is stretched
For warriors' death.
The weft in the loom
Drips with blood.
The battle darkens.
Under our fingers
The tapestry grows,
Red as heart's blood,
Blue as corpses,
The web of battle.

What is this woof?
The guts of men,
The weights on the warp
Their slaughtered heads. . . .

With swords for shuttles
The war-web we weave,
Valkyries weaving
The web of victory. . . .

Many Orkneymen followed their earl, Sigurd, to the dynastic battle fought on Good Friday, 1014, at Clontarf in Ireland.

Sigurd is the name of our earl.
His mother the witch
Wove our black banner. The raven
Streams and flaps above the host.
Who bears that bird of victory
Drinks tonight in dark halls.
Now Sigurd, alone,
Offers the raven to a sackcloth sun.

*

I forget the name of the saint
That saved my grandfather
Under the walls of Paris one summer.
Whatever your name is, white one,
I am grandson
To old Olaf, that you kept from torrents of
lead and tar,
One day in a French siege.
I will light candles for you.

*

Midhowe Broch, Rousay:
Evie across the Sound

I bought the horse in Dublin.
Seven times
It reared against horn and shield wall.
Now the horse is hide and bone,
I am walking back to the town.
At the river mouth
The proud Minch-trampler is moored.

*

Coming to Ireland
We stopped first at Barra.
A cold week, snow in the ale.
Coming to Ireland
About some royal mix-up or other,
We stopped next at Man.
Coming to Ireland
We have stopped at this noisy fairground.
There seems to be no road out of it.

*

I drank thick ale in Galloway.
Battles, blood, wall-breaching –
Bravely I boasted!
Now the glory is come
There is no ditch anywhere
I would not creep into,
Sharing a mushroom with tramp or slut.

The most fascinating insight into the complex nature of those Norse Orkneymen is provided by the 'Jerusalem-farers' chapters in *Orkneyinga Saga*. The fifteen ships of Earl Rognvald Kolson set out on a crusade – 'pilgrimage' would be a more accurate description, since there were no infidels to fight at that particular time (1151–54). This God-faring may be seen as an act of penance done on behalf of an entire people, to redeem a savage history, to turn over the page scarred with red and write words of grace on the new white parchment. But pirates don't become saints overnight. Between Scapa and the domes of Jerusalem the cold-eyed seamen dallied for months in the port of Narbonne, and the earl fell in love, in the courtly fashion of the time, with the countess Ermengarde. His mouth brimmed with skaldic verse that must have sounded barbarous in the ear of a girl attuned to the bird-notes and fragrances and exquisite shapes of Provençal verse.

They broke at last out of the honeyed web of Narbonne, and came half-starved to a port in Galicia. The townsfolk refused to open their stores to them, for, said they, they had little to give – the Castle on the hill seized all the grapes and olives and fish that they had reaped by their labour. In the cold and hunger of mid-winter the pilgrims reduced the Castle to a smoking ruin; and, judging by the *Saga*, they did their old pagan work with style and relish.

With style and relish, too, a few months later, they surrounded and captured and burned a Moslem merchant-ship, a large 'dromond'. Out of the side of the flaming ship flowed, like honey, streams of molten gold. The black captain said he would rather the sea had his treasure than the Vikings. His wit and courage saved him. The pilgrims set him ashore safe at his own port.

At every landfall they fought and got drunk and were the kind of men they had always been.

A hundred swords were broken that voyage.
Prayer on a hundred white wings
Rose every morning. The Mediterranean
Was richer by a hundred love songs.

Into the tapestry of blood and guts were gathered all the same, and for the first time, rose and dove and palm-branch.

King Hakon of Norway with a great fleet arrived in Orkney in 1263. His mission was to reassert Norway's sovereignty over those parts of Scotland that had for so long been within the circle of Norwegian influence. Slowly, that Scandinavian influence had been eroding as Scotland became ever more aware of itself as a nation. King Hakon's fleet sailed down the west coast. A storm threw some of his ships against the coast, near Largs. Round those ships the battle was fought, without any clear-cut decision. But the eye of history saw it as a Scottish victory, for the old snow king sailed north again; and that was the last time a Norse king threatened Scotland. In Orkney the king sickened. As death approached the priests read to him from the Latin scriptures. Later, in the Bishop's Palace where he lay, he asked for the sagas of his ancestors to be read to him. His body lay that winter in St Magnus Cathedral.

Eventually not only the Western Isles but Orkney and Shetland became part of Scotland, in fulfilment of the marriage contract between King James III of Scotland and a Danish princess. The islands were pledged for a huge sum of money, which in fact was never paid. For the Norn-speaking Orkney people it must have been a difficult time. New alien laws threatened their ancient udal tenures. Increasingly Scotsmen were brought into positions of power. Orcadians remembered the authority and influence that Orkney had once held in the counsels of the north; now it was only a remote province of Scotland, open for any Scottish adventurer or sycophant to strip and despoil. Eventually it came to armed rebellion. King James V sent from Caithness, under the command of Lord William St Clair, a royal punitive force. At a place called Summerdale, on the borders of Orphir and Stenness, the Orkney rebels swarmed out of the hills and cut the Caithness army to pieces. Only one Orkney boy was killed, and that by his own mother; he had stripped the uniform from a dead Caithness soldier and was returning home under the first stars; the mother, having heard all day the thunder of battle among the hills, assumed that the royal army had been victorious, and that her son was probably wounded to death or hanged; she filled a long stocking with stones and struck the oncoming green-clad figure again and again until he was dead.

Later, King James visited Orkney, and his presence patched up a peace that was never seriously threatened again.

One troop of young Orkneymen followed Montrose in his last campaign against Cromwell and the Parliament. At Carbiesdale in the Highlands they were crushed by well-armed professional troops; it's said that not one found his way back to Orkney.

Only the Orkney lairds showed any enthusiasm for the Jacobite Rebellion of 1745. After Culloden, many of them spent miserable months hiding in a cave in Westray, still known as Gentlemen's Ha'.

The long wars of the eighteenth century brought much shipping and wealth into Orkney, especially to the growing town of Stromness. The later Napoleonic wars brought terror to many an Orkney croft. The great men-of-war were constantly in need of seamen. In Orkney, as in every other maritime place, the 'press-gang' were busy. If young men did not volunteer for the offered bounty money, they were seized in the fields and fishing-nousts. Many of them never saw the islands again. There is a treasury of press-gang stories, in which a constant theme is the outwitting of the press-gang by sweethearts and mothers of the young men sought.

French and American privateers swarmed everywhere in those days and were a constant menace to British merchant ships. The island of Hoy in Orkney has its Martello defensive towers, but it seems they never uttered thunder and flame. (Of all the hundreds of Martello towers, the only one to gain fame is the one James Joyce lived in at Sandymount, Dublin, in 1904.)

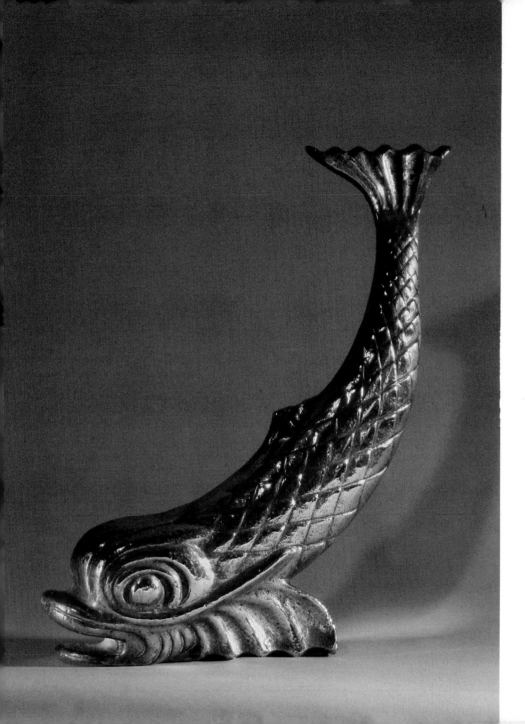

In 1914 the main naval base of the British Navy was Scapa Flow, the wide stretch of sea enclosed by the southern Mainland shore and the south islands of Orkney, yet giving easy access to the Atlantic and the North Sea. Out of Scapa Flow the *Hampshire* sailed one stormy June day in 1916, carrying Lord Kitchener on his way to Russia for military talks. Off Marwick Head in Birsay the warship struck a mine and went down. Only a handful of men survived out of eight or nine hundred. Kitchener with his cold 'your-country-needs-you' eye was one with pearl and coral.

Out of Scapa Flow also sailed the British Fleet to challenge the German Grand Fleet at Jutland in 1916 – the battle that was claimed as a victory by both sides.

In Scapa Flow in June 1919 the same surrendered German Grand Fleet committed suicide. At a given signal the cocks were opened and one by one the huge ships heeled over. The intricate and technically difficult salvage of them was, between the two wars, a major industry in Orkney; the steel of the German warships was of the highest quality.

Again, in 1939, the British Navy sought the security of Scapa Flow. A few weeks after the war started a daring U-boat commander, Günther Prien, entered Scapa Flow through Water Sound and drove torpedoes into H.M.S. *Royal Oak* lying under the sea-cliffs of Holm. Again hundreds of young sailors were killed. A buoy marks the place where the great ship and her crew have their sea burial. Prien went home to a hero's welcome, and received the Iron Cross from Hitler himself. Later he went down with his U-boat.

Ornament from the *Royal Oak* sunk in Scapa Flow, 1939 (*Stromness Museum*)

A block-ship: sunk in the Second World War to seal an entry into Scapa Flow

For the first time for centuries Orkney was actually in the front line of war: in the dark of the moon squadrons of German bombers probed the defences of Scapa Flow again and again. The circle of seeking searchlights, the vivid pandemonium of the anti-aircraft guns, the faint undulant drone of the German bombers made high dangerous drama for the Orcadians of 1940 and 1941. Over the little hamlet of Brig-o-Waithe, between the sea and the Loch of Stenness, a fleeing bomber scattered its incendiaries. A villager standing in his doorway was killed, others were injured – they were the first British civilian casualties of the war.

In those days Orkney was crammed with garrison troops. They outnumbered the island folk probably by three to one. In the centre of the main island were two fighter aerodromes, at Skeabrae and Twatt. So far from there being any friction between servicemen and islanders, there was such harmony throughout those five years that many ex-soldiers and airmen return this summer or that; as in the First World War, too, there were scores of marriages between servicemen and Orkney girls, and as often as not they settled in the islands, and begot a new generation of Orcadians.

All that massive expenditure of energy and money was for the defence of Scapa Flow. There is not very much to show for it now. But one piece of defence has, over the years, become an indispensable feature of Orkney: the Churchill barriers built, after Prien and the *Royal Oak*, to seal the eastern gates into Scapa Flow.

The scarlet threads of war are plentiful in the history of Orkney. What Orcadians hope now is that the tapestry will grow with peaceful natural greens and blues; another war would put an end forever to the threads and the loom and the patient weaving hands.

Hoy, cloud-tangled,
from the shore of the big island

Earl Patrick Stewart's palace, Kirkwall: 'possibly
the most mature and accomplished piece of
Renaissance architecture left in Scotland'

Culture 10

ORKNEY LITERATURE goes back for hundreds of years. We still
have the stories and poems that the Iceland and Orkney skalds
recited, especially at the cultured court of Earl Rognvald Kolson,
himself an outstanding poet (apart from his other accomplish-
ments):

> *Chessboard, tiltyard, trout-stream*
> *Know my sweet passes.*
> *Old writings are no mystery to me*
> *Nor any modern book.*
> *Ski across winterfold flashes.*
> *Deep curves I make with arrow and oar.*
> *I know the twelve notes of a harp.*
> *At the red forge*
> *My clamorous shadow is sometimes rooted.*

No doubt the Celtic broch-builders, those ingenious folk, had
an oral tradition of poetry and story, but the language is lost, and
with it the jewels of the language. Further back in history, the
men who had the imagination and skill to build Maeshowe
would also have used their talents to quarry and dress and
pattern the hard stone of language. That is lost also; we can enter
their world only through the imagination:

> *I tell you, he whose burnt bones*
> *Are in this jar*
> *Was loved by the people.*
> *But the girl Bertha*

> *Wept different tears from the tears of*
> *children and elders.*
>
> *'I have longed often*
> *For the fire and this funeral jar'*
>
> *This man turned the great ox horns*
> *Into the eye of the sun*

Though it was an Icelander who put together *Orkneyinga Saga*,
no doubt he was but one master among hundreds of good boreal
story-tellers. The story-telling tradition continued in Orkney
until the mid-nineteenth century; newspapers, radio, television
have killed the last of that folk art.

At all times and in all places, probably, official art and popular
art exist side by side. The earl's skalds made noble victory-songs,
resounding elegies. It is possible to imagine 'the ditch poets'
giving the other side of the story.

> *We say this of the chief –*
> *Better his mother*
> *Had herded geese, milked goats*
> *Than bided his nine moons.*

The art of narrative and poetry went underground with the
Scots ascendancy. The people remembered, possibly in corrupt
ways, some of the great northern poems. (Their Norn tongue was
unregarded and discouraged.) There is the well-known episode
of the eighteenth-century North Ronaldsay minister who

received a new-printed copy of Thomas Gray's poems, including the paraphrase 'The Fatal Sisters'. He read that poem aloud one night in the manse to some of his parishioners. He hadn't got very far when they interrupted him. They knew that poem well in the original Norse, out of *The Story of Burnt Njal*.*

The popular poetry passed, from mouth to ear: word-patterns of things that intrigued or delighted them: riddles, proverbs, spells against pest and sickness. A few have survived, recorded in John Firth's remarkable book and elsewhere. But in general the centuries between Largs and Waterloo are dumb and blank; the only written things are a few land-rolls, rentals, processes, wills out of lawyers' offices and lairds' chests. But the ancient legends and lore were recited still around the hearth-stones; those first attempts to make beautiful and meaningful 'the burthen of the mystery' of life. How many of those treasures were lost in the transition from Norn to Orcadian Scots? It must have been a difficult time for more than one generation of storytellers. Many of these minglings of the supernatural and the fabulous are preserved in local lore. Those who wish to study the subject could do no better than read Ernest W. Marwick's recent *Folklore of Orkney and Shetland*.

Books began to be printed in Orkney in the nineteenth century. Country boys and girls learned in the new-built schools the rudiments of reading and writing. Some of them in later years wrote down their thoughts in verse – generally, after the fashion of the day, faded melancholy whimsical lyrics, void of the dark earth-strength of the popular word-art that was disapproved of by dominie and minister. Yet, with reading and writing (in 1872 universal education was a legal requirement) an innate intelligence asserted itself, and in less than fifty years Orkneymen produced hundreds of valuable books, on every conceivable subject: religion, geology, lore, history, language, place-names, agriculture, travel, memoir, archaeology, nature.

A Sanday farmer called Walter Traill Dennison published dialect stories of great perception and humour in the mid-nineteenth century; he also saved from oblivion much of the traditional lore. But perhaps his best claim to fame is that he pieced together a magnificent ballad called *The Play o' Da Lathie Odivere*; which southern ballad anthologists, overmuch taken up with the achievements in that genre of the wandering bards of the Borders and the north-east, have neglected for too long. Was that great story of the seal-king and his human lover first recited in one of the Stuart halls of Birsay or Kirkwall?

The imagination of Orcadians who were growing up towards the end of the last century was quickened by new translations of the Icelandic sagas. The local historian John Mooney tells how he read for the first time, entranced, a translation of *Orkneyinga Saga* (it may have been Dasent's, or the Anderson edition) lying on a summer afternoon at the sea-banks of Scapa. It was like the young Keats first looking into Chapman's *Homer*. . . . Up to that time those who wrote about the islands (mainly ministers) allude vaguely to the fact that they were once governed by 'Danish counts', portentous figures lost in a Gothic fog. Now here, at last, was the true ancient island story, steeped in light, and overbrimming with what the human mind hungers for, especially in a drab confining commercial age that tends increasingly to reduce life to a cipher – bravery, loyalty, far-voyaging, the heroic coming to terms with inexorable fate.

An Orkneyman, Samuel Laing, was one of the first translators of Icelandic saga, and his renderings are still widely admired.

---

*See 'The warp is stretched' fragment on page 92.

A smithy in Evie

It seems that those literary discoveries may well have been responsible for the quickening of the Orkney creative imagination that followed soon afterwards. Perhaps the most important writer (though, strangely, he showed little signs of having read the saga literature) was Edwin Muir (1887–1959), poet, critic, translator. His poetry has the profundity and visionary quality of myth – it seems to tap deep unapprehended sources, going back countless generations to the very roots. His symbols are immediately recognisable to a sensitive island reader; they seem to come out of a deep communal unconscious mind, old buried treasures that the poet has dug up; mysterious life-giving symbols. Muir's poetry is quiet on the surface, like a tarn in the hills; yet we know instinctively that there are lucent mysterious depths. The rhythms and movement of the verse suggest the long fluent laterals of the islands; it is as if the natural shapes all about him had passed into the heart and mind of Muir in his childhood:

> Long time he lay upon the sunny hill,
> To his father's house below securely bound.
> Far off the silent, changing sound was still,
> With the black islands lying thick around. . . .
>
> Over the sound a ship so slow would pass
> That in the black hill's gloom it seemed to lie.
> The evening sound was smooth like sunken glass,
> And time seemed finished ere the ship passed by.
>
> Gray tiny rocks slept round him where he lay,
> Moveless as they, more still as evening came,
> The grasses threw straight shadows far away,
> And from the house his mother called his name.

The novels of Eric Linklater (1899–1974) go back in spirit to the sagamen: they have the same largeness and vigour. Many a middle-aged Orcadian learned to love the islands first through the medium of Linklater's prose narrative: Orkney had once been great – the people in *White-Maa's Saga* and *Magnus Merriman* still live the full instinctive gay life of voyagers and first settlers. To the bareness of saga he added an Elizabethan richness. His prose rises again and again into the intensity of poetry:

> The lake is subject to the sky, and about those northern islands the sky, from day to day, is a drunken hooligan, a dance of Cupids, a rout of silver-breasted Cuirassiers, a weeping savage, or a temple for the Princess of China. The lake replies. As well as water may, it echoes gaiety and gloom, youth in its morning rage, beauty in her pride or naked in her innocence. It has no constant quality. In winter it will drown its green islets, in summer its banks are hidden by meadowsweet and flags.
> It is quick with many birds, with mallard and merganser and the black-headed gull. A tight rabble of coots rising in sudden alarm, with staccato clapping of their wings, will scuttle in a crystal storm for the shelter of a bay. In June comes idly sailing a fleet of swans, and that exquisite warrior, the Arctic tern, hangs like a hawk in the unmoving air. . . .

Robert Rendall (1897–1967) was a Kirkwall draper who, towards the end of his life, produced a handful of marvellous lyrics in the Orkney dialect. They have the perfection and purity of *The Greek Anthology* (some of them are translations from it) but Rendall's poems are steeped in cold boreal light:

> The winter lift is glintan doun
> Wi' tullimentan stars besprent,
> As were the very heavens abune
> Clean gyte wi frosty merriment,
> Their lowan e'en are taakan tent
> O' chiels like Mansie o' the Bu

Whase days upon the land are spent
Ruggan wi' Taurus and the Pleugh.

Speaking for myself, I admit to being intrigued by Orkney's 'lost centuries', the men and women and the things that happened then: pirates, smugglers, witches, lairds, ministers, factors, ploughmen and fishermen. It is as if the tongue wished to make of that long blankness and silence a meaning and a celebration.

There has been a fine flowering in art and painting and design in Orkney in the last century. Very little had happened in that mode since the Picts – except a few crude strong anonymous woodcuts of this remarkable place and that (Palace of Birsay, Maeshowe, etc.) – until in the eighteenth century a Kirkwall man called Robert Strange made a national name for himself as an engraver, generally of the classics of renaissance art. But the coming of cheap easy reproduction meant that artists like Strange were quickly forgotten.

There was also a Stenness man called Charles Smith of Tormiston who actually became 'painter to the Great Mogul', Shah Allum. He had studied at the Royal Academy under Sir Joshua Reynolds.

The Daniell brothers did a striking series of engraved prints of Orkney in the 1820s, touched with the romance and stage-setting of the times. The public demanded of their artists that the commonplace be made to yield all its latent remarkable qualities; which is possibly why artists not of the top class had to resort so often to the dramatic or the fanciful. (There is in one Daniell print a plume of cloud across the summit of Ward Hill, Hoy, that just *could* be a volcano.) These Daniell prints were probably the only local pictures to hang in Orkney parlours until early this century. Now Orkney, after the fine example of Stanley Cursiter, Queen's Limner, is full of good artists – Ian MacInnes, Sylvia Wishart, Ian Scott, Edgar Gibson, Nancy Ramsay, John Crossley, Marion Ashburn, Stuart Sim, Keith Laird, Sandy Young, Erlend Brown, Lesley Johns, Fiona MacInnes, and many more. There is rarely a week when there is not an exhibition by a local artist showing in the Kirkwall Library. Within the last year, in Stromness, the Pier Arts Centre has been opened, a beautiful gallery where, among a permanent collection of the St Ives school, artists from Orkney and elsewhere exhibit their works.

Mention must also be made of Margaret Tait, maker of beautiful films, who is also a talented poet and story-teller; and of Bessie Skea, a lyrical essayist; and such photographers as Gunnie Moberg and Charles Tait and Chick Chalmers – all artists of talent.

If there was any original Orkney music – and there must have been – it is even more lost than the ballads and tales. Before the Reformation there was a 'sang school' attached to St Magnus Cathedral, where no doubt the boy choristers learned Latin and polyphony and other subjects. A fragment of an early *Hymn to St Magnus* lies in the library of Uppsala University, Sweden. There must have been many others composed in the islands by Orkney musicians.

The popular music of fiddles and pipes must, we assume, have gone on continuously; except when, here and there, and for a brief period, a puritanical minister put his foot through the lyrical strings. But the unique Orkney music that must have been has, in the past two centuries or so, been shouldered out by Scottish modes. Strathspey and reel are enormously popular in the islands. Canned music – record player and radio – has not at all diminished the number of Orkney fiddlers and accordianists. . . .

Fiddler to farm-girls, a reel,
A rose,
A tumult of opening circles.

Some excellent songs – lyrics and melodies – have been written of late by local composers, like Ally Windwick.

Drama and classical music have a wide following in the islands; what is more important, people actively participate. The Drama Festival each February brings together one-act plays (sometimes locally written) from all over Orkney. The School of Music in Stromness is a regular feature of the late summer, when the Orkney children, their skills tempered by expert tuition, perform classical and new music with great enthusiasm. The Scottish Arts Council does not neglect the islands; sponsored by it and the local Arts Society, professional musicians regularly come north.

A recently naturalised Orcadian is the composer Peter Maxwell Davies, who lives much of the year in a high lonely cottage in Rackwick, Hoy. He gladly acknowledges that living in Orkney has given him new themes and inspiration for his already internationally acclaimed music. He found the fragmentary *Hymn to St Magnus* at Uppsala, and wove into it the gales, sea-surge, cliff-echoes, silences, of the beautiful valley where he lives.

Rackwick

Model in Stromness Museum of the paddle-steamer *Royal Mail* —mid-19th century— first steamer on the Stromness–Scrabster passage

The Standing Stones of Stenness:
four erect monoliths dating from
the early bronze age

Lore 11

WHY IS IT that sea water is salt, and the water of burn and well sweet? What are the standing stones – the great circle on the moor and the smaller groups and the individual stones in this field and that? Why are some people ugly, or unlucky all their lives? What are those green mounds and humps here and there in the islands, that look so mysterious on a summer evening late? What are the stars and meteors and planets? Why should certain patterns of sound – music – make the feet want to dance round with the sun? Why does the corn come up green and thick one summer, and sickly the next summer? There is the ruddy ripening sun of June, and the pale wick of December.

Folk-lore – the stories that a people have cherished over many generations and centuries, and recited again and again across the winter fires – is no collection of idle whimsy, vanities spun to pass the time between supper and bed. They are attempts to come to terms with certain mysterious matters in a people's surroundings and circumstances – to explain things which would otherwise be baffling and therefore hostile. The tales have roots deep in the earliest folk-memory. They might seem to be 'a lot of old bruck and nonsense' to the modern forward-looking number-orientated Orkneyman, but the stories are a part of him whether he likes it or not, and he ignores what Edwin Muir called 'the fable' at his peril. (Science explains the old mysteries, in ever greater detail, but in a cold factual rootless way.)

Here then is why the sea came to be salt. The sea was sweet as the springs and burns when the sea-king captured from the royal palace of Denmark the two giant slave girls Fenia and Menia, along with the mill Grotti which ground out between its ponderous stones whatever you told it to produce: gold or soldiers or roses. Only the huge strength of Fenia and Menia could turn the querns. Somewhere in the North Sea, the prow set fair for the Pentland Firth between Caithness and Orkney, the sea-king ordered Grotti to make salt. The monstrous girls put their shoulders to the stone, and salt gushed out. Probably the sea-king only wanted a little salt to sprinkle on the rib of beef he was eating, but Grotti spewed out salt and laboured to set more hills of salt on the deck of the ship, and frosted the beard of the sea-king. The ship, burdened with salt, teetered and sank in the Pentland Firth, but down below the mill Grotti turns forever. In the Pentland Firth is a whirlpool called The Swelkie: thirled forever to Grotti on the sea bed.

People disappear now and then. If a known person disappears nowadays you inform the police, employ an agency, insert an appeal in a newspaper; because, of course, in our common-sense age, there must be some simple factual explanation of the disappearance: the Foreign Legion, the lure of the gay life of London, simple boredom.

A Rousay girl disappeared long ago. One day, years later, her father and brothers were at sea fishing when a fog came down and shrouded them. They were lost. But soon, through the solid gray and the gray whirls, they sighted land and rowed towards it. They secured their boat and walked up to a house above the shore. They had never been in this island before. The woman of the house took them in and gave them food and drink. The brothers did not know who the woman was, but the father recognised his daughter. She told him that a seal-man had taken her to the vanishing island of Hether-Blether, and now she was his wife and quite happy with him and her sea-children. . . .

A young man took home to his old parents a strange cold girl. He told them he had fallen in love with her and was going to marry her. The young ones married in the kirk and had children. The old ones died, this winter or that. The hard work of the croft went on, a monotonous necessary cycle of labour, year after year. The croft-wife made cheese and bannocks and butter, rocked the cradle, looked to the hearth-fire, kept the water buckets brimming. Then one day she went away as suddenly as she had come. She was never seen again. Her deserted man, when he looked one day among his barn rafters, saw that the seal-pelt he kept there had vanished – the skin he had taken from a rock the very night he led home to his parents the girl whose vowels when she spoke were cold sea sounds.

The standing stones are sun-stricken giants. Orkney was full of giants in those days, violent argumentative monsters. The earth shook when they moved. They hurled vast rocks at each other. Cubbie Roo was a giant in the island of Wyre. Mothers in the last century would warn their ill-answering children: 'Cubbie Roo'll get thee!' But in fact Cubbie Roo is a folk-version of an actual historical figure, Kolbein Hruga the laird of Wyre in Norse times. Kolbein Hruga must have been a formidable man indeed, so to be invested with the huge girth and trappings of legend.

A giant who lived in Scotland decided to build a new house. He came to Orkney to get stones and earth. With three vast steps he splashed his way across the Pentland Firth. He scooped two fistfuls of earth from the Mainland and put them in the cubbie (straw basket) that he carried on his shoulder. He turned for home. Some of the soil spilled from his basket into the sea.

Another step, and the basket-strap broke: all the earth fell into the sea with an almighty splash! The two grooves in the Mainland soon filled with water from burns and underground springs; they became the Loch of Stenness and the Loch of Harray. The first soil spilling from the giant's cubbie became the little green island of Graemsay; the second dollop became Hoy with its dark hills and cliffs.

Trows lived in the green mounds or howes that occur everywhere in the islands. Often they were evil beings who did mischief to croft and croft folk. Even today, if a person has been sick for a time, he is said to be 'trowie' – that is, the trows have smitten him. The trows sought always to exchange their own ugly deformed offspring for human children, and sometimes they succeeded; and that is the reason why some folk are uglier, awkwarder, more misshapen than others. At midwinter the trows were especially active; reading the old accounts one has the impression that every little isolated bewintered croft was sieged, between sunset and dawn, by dark malevolent hordes. Special words had to be uttered over the farm-implements, ploughs and querns. All actions had to be performed sun-wise: withershins was the way of witch and trow. Lintel and bed had to be 'sained', at first with a cross, and later with a bible: the trows had no power over those holy symbols.

But possibly there were good helpful under-earth creatures too: they kept the wells pure and sweet, they sent up the corn into the ripening sun and rain and wind. They didn't of course do

Box-bed and vessels used in Orkney farms in earlier times. The wooden vessel is a 'cog'. Filled with a hot potent mixture of ale and spirits, it would be passed round at weddings from hand to hand and mouth to mouth.
(*Tankerness House Museum*)

these kindnesses for nothing. What they loved most about human beings were the patterns they made, especially their sound-patterns: music. So they would linger, drunk with reels, at every barn door where there was a wedding reception or a harvest home.

The strangest of all the old legends concerns the two fiddlers returning home late on a summer night from a country wedding. The road led them past a cluster of those green 'knowes' which were known to be the dwelling-places of trows. The young fiddlers, perhaps a little drunk with the wedding ale, conversed with each other, their voices loud and high in the glimmering summer stillness. Suddenly one of the fiddlers beame aware that he was getting no answers; he turned; his friend was not there. Then fiddle music flashed out from the heart of the knowe. The solitary fiddler ran home in terror, clutching his varnished silent bird to his breast. . . . Years later this same fiddler, with wrinkles at the eyes and ash in his beard now, was walking along the same road on a summer midnight when he became aware of a strange but familiar footstep beside him. He turned; he recognised with a pang the fiddler who had disappeared so long ago. The young man had aged not a single hour; he had the apples in his face and his beard was untarnished gold.

The mind delights to linger on this beautiful story. Under the surface pattern, the old story-teller seems to be speculating on the nature of art: what we mean when we say that, at its best, all creative art is 'timeless'. In their chamber under the hill the trows had asked the stolen fiddler – after he had tasted their delicious meat and drink – to play one tune for them; then they would let him go. After what seemed ten minutes or so the fiddler was out under the summer stars again. But in fact twenty-five harvests had been sown and reaped (or ten harvests, or a hundred, according to different versions).

> *'Darst thu gang b' the black furrow*
> *This night, thee and thy song? . . .'*

> *'Weet me mooth wi' the Lenten ale,*
> *I'll go along.'*

> *They spied him near the black furrow*
> *B' the glim o' the wolf star.*
> *Slow the dance was in his feet,*
> *Dark the fiddle he bore. . . .*

> *There stood three men at the black furrow*
> *And one was clad in green.*
> *They've taen the fiddler b' the hand*
> *Where he was no more seen. . . .*

> *They've put the gowd cup in his hand,*
> *Elfin bread on his tongue.*
> *There he bade a hundred years*
> *Him and his lawless song. . . .*

Perhaps indeed fertility is the root of the story. Was it in a summertime of poor corn that the fiddler was dragged down into the earth? Was his song meant to purify choked and polluted sources? The old story-teller may well have been upholding the dignity of all those who 'make things beautiful and good'. A tale or a statue or a song is not made to give a moment's fleeting pleasure to superior cultured minds; they are absolutely necessary for the well-being and health of a community. Without good art – vision – a people perishes.

> Art must be of *use* – a coercive rhyme, to strand a whale
> on the rock, a scratch on stone to make the corn grow.
> What are all those fiddles and statues and books for? . . .

The interior of Hoy
—'the high island'

Binscarth, near Finstown:
one of the few sylvan places in Orkney

A Nature Anthology 12

THERE IS such a great wealth of books, over the last century or so, on the natural history of Orkney, in all its aspects, that any précis would be the barest skeleton. (To write an essay on the subject would only reveal this writer's profound ignorance.) What might be of interest is to discover man's changing relationship with his environment and fellow-creatures over the centuries from Jo Ben's giants and monsters and miracles of the early sixteenth century, through the benign eye that Rev James Wallace turned on nature a century and a half later, to Rev George Barry's huge scientific catalogue of 1805, which yet contains much fresh and delightfully-phrased observation. I hope that this approach to the subject will add another dimension to the book: to look at Orkney through contemporary eyes alone amounts, in a way, to distortion, for other times have seen it quite differently, and there is nothing like the prose of another age to bring that time to full and vivid life. Most of Jo Ben's monsters have vanished; so, alas, have some of the birds mentioned by Wallace and Barry. But most remain, and the photographs in this book reveal our land creatures and birds in all their swift delicate unique beauty.

Hardly a thing is known about Jo Ben. The name itself is strange – possibly a contracted form of John Bellenden. The tradition is that he was an ecclesiastic of some kind. His manuscript *Descriptio Insularum Orchadearum* (1529) is in the Advocates' Library, Edinburgh.

It seems unlikely that he visited every island; at any rate, some are given much fuller treatment than others.

North Ronaldsay
In the north part of the island large native animals (selchies) are captured in nets made of hemp, and there is also there a large rock, called Selchskerry, where sea fowl live and nest.... The people of the island interchanging grumbles among themselves at delays coming in the way, approach the rock with large hazel sticks. At first the animals, eyeing them with anger and gnashing of teeth, strive to move away with wide open mouths: then they attack with all their strength.... If the first beast escapes without injury, all the others attack the men with their teeth, but if the first fall and die, all the others take to flight and are easily captured....

Sanday
English and German vessels often meet with destruction in one part of the island, towards the east, called the Har of Lopness. I myself, passing through this island, being fatigued, rested myself at a church called the Holy Cross, and in the churchyard saw innumerable skulls of men, about a thousand, larger than the heads of any living tribe (or larger than three heads of those now living), and I extracted teeth from the gums of the size of a hazel nut.... Rabbits are abundant in summer, and in winter are so tame that they are taken into houses....

Stronsay

A great monster, called Troicis, often associates with women living here. When I resided there a beautiful woman that was married to an able-bodied farmer, was much tormented by a great spirit and both were seen, against the husband's will, lying on one bed. The woman at last became emaciated with sorrow. I advised that she might get freedom by prayer, almsgiving, and fasting: the duration of her trouble lasted a year. The description of the monster is this: he was covered with seaweed over his whole body, and resembled a dark horse with wrinkled skin, with limbs like a horse.

Auskerry

Another uncultivated island, where the horses are very ferocious.

Faray

The meaning of the name is the beautiful or pleasant isle. It is very suitable for animals, especially cows, which there graze on bushes with great satisfaction, and the boys sing to the dull beasts. The whole island is plentiful of corn and fishes.

Eynhallow

It is of old times related that here, if the standing corn be cut down after the setting of the sun, unexpectedly there is a flowing of blood from the stalks of the grain; also it is said that if a horse is fastened after sundown, it will easily get loose.

Eday

There is a great abundance of cattle. The men sometimes fight with great monsters, which they cut up in dregs (or melt the dregs into fat), then boil and cook into oil.

Damsay

No frogs, toads, or other noxious terrestrial creatures are found here. The women here are sterile, and if they do become pregnant never bring forth with life.

Deerness

This parish of old times was wooded and many wild beasts were found here: at length, floods coming, the trees were uprooted and were submerged.

St Olai

The women here are given to excess in luxuries and pleasures; this is supposed to be caused by the abundance of fish obtainable. Here is a very high mountain named Whitford.

Stenhouse

In this parish there is a large lake, 24 miles in circuit. On a little hill near the lake in a tomb was found the bones of a man in length 14 feet, and money was found under the head of the dead man.

Seals on the beach at North Ronaldsay

Stromness

Beneficial winds here blow called Etesian for about forty days every year about the dog days. Here is a very dangerous bridge for travellers, called the Bridge of Vaith, where many perish.

Pomona

All the men are very drunken and wanton, and fight among themselves. For an example of their friendship, if one neighbour invites another and if the invited before his departure has not vomited he assails his host and there is much strife. . . .

Jo Ben, if he was a wandering friar, lingered still in the dim region between fantasy and nature. The Rev James Wallace saw wonders everywhere too, but the wonders he contemplated and wrote about are in the order of nature. It can be inferred, too, that he was a kindlier man than Jo Ben; it would have been pleasant to sit with him in his rectory at Sanday and (later) Kirkwall, and share a bowl of hot punch with him on a winter evening. He flourished when the tides of religious establishment in Scotland fluctuated between Episcopalianism and Presbyterianism. He himself was a bishop's man, but nothing of the rage of the period stains his serene pages.

A Stone from the Clouds

The Air and Clouds here, by the Operation of the Sun do sometime generate several things, for Instance some few years hence some Fishermen Fishing half a League from land, over against *Copinsha*, in a fair Day there fell down from the Air a Stone about the bigness of a Football, which fell in the midst of the Boat, and Sprung a Lake in it, to the great hazard of the lives of the men that were in it, which could be no other but some substance generated in the Clouds. The Stone was like condensed or Petrified Clay. . . .

Ice in Summer

Sometimes the Rains descend not by drops but by Spouts of Water, as if whole Clouds fell down at once. About Four years ago, after a great thunder in the Moneth of *June*, there fell a great Flake of Ice, more than a Foot thick.

The Teeming Earth

This Countrey abounds with variety both of Field and Garden Plants, Especially Cabbage, Turnipe, Parsnipe, Carrot, Crummock, Artichock, grow to a greater bigness here than I have seen them else where. I have seen Strawberries that would be three inch about, sometimes the Herbs are monstrously fruitful, for out of the flower of a Marigold, I have seen twelve more growing; the like I have seen in the wild Deasie. . . .

Sheepdead

The Sheep usually die of a Disease called the *Sheepdead*, which is occasioned by great quantities of little Animals like to Flouks of an inch long, which are engendered in the Liver. I put one of them in a Microscope, and found it like a little Flouk wanting finns.

Horses, Swine, Rabbits, Snails

The Horses are but little, Yet strong and well mettald, most of which they get from *Zetland*, and are called *Shelties*. There are great herds of Swine, and rich cuningars almost in every Isle, well stored with Rabbets. . . . There is a great Snail that hath a bright white stone growing in it.

Trees

There is no Forrest or Wood in all this Country, nor any Trees, except some that are in the Bishop's Garden at *Kirkwall*, where are some Ashes and thorn and Plum-Trees. . . . Yet it seems there hath been Woods growing in this Country, for in the Mosses they find Trees with their Branches intire of 20 or 30 foot length.

Waters

This Countrey being divided in small Islands, it cannot be expected there should be in it any Rivers, yet there is every where a great many Bourns and torrents, well replenished with Trouts, both small and great, some of them like to young Salmon.

There is a large Loch in the *Mainland*, called the Loch of *Stennis*, but unfruitful. . . . The Loch of *Swanna* in the *Mainland*, will have in some parts a thick scumm of Copper Colour upon it, which makes some think there is some Mine under it.

Nothing much is known either about Dr George Barry, minister of Shapinsay. In 1805 he published in Edinburgh his massive *The History of the Orkney Islands: in which is comprehended an Account of their Present as well as their Ancient State; together with The Advantages they Possess for Several Branches of Industry, and the Means by which they may be Improved. Illustrated With an Accurate and Extensive Map of the Whole Islands, and With Plates of some of the most Interesting Objects they contain.*

Wallace's attempt to see Orkney as a whole is a frail web compared to the massive monument erected by the scholarship of Barry; in little more than a century so much more information had accumulated. Barry was one of a scholarly group of Orkney Presbyterian ministers which included Rev George Low (Birsay) and Dr Charles Clouston (Sandwick).

The century of reason had intervened between Wallace and Barry; some of the wonder has gone, but still Barry writes about the flora and fauna of the islands with charm and fluency, and with the exactitude and authority of the new science. Of his long catalogue there is space to quote only a very brief selection.

A Lead Mine

Near the manse of Stromness, which is about a mile to the westward of the town, there may be seen, embedded in a rock consisting of schistose clay, Lydian stone, which it contains in its cavities filled with bitumen; and, on the adjacent shore, in a rock immediate between schistose and indurated clay, many pieces of galena.

Struck with the flattering appearance of these, men of skill in mineralogy were induced to inspect the place with accuracy; and as they judged it probable that lead might be found there in abundance, a company of miners were employed, who wrought for some time, but were at length compelled to desist, being convinced that all the metal which they could procure, would not be adequate to the expence of the labour.

The Garden

In the flower-garden, the rose, the tulip, the carnation, the pink, the primrose, with a multitude of other flowers, are cultivated with success; while the kitchen garden produces cabbage, broccoli, cauliflower, peas, beans, spinach, onions, leeks, parsley, cresses, beets, lettuces, turnips, carrots, parsnips, celery, and artichokes; all of which are good of their kind, but particularly the last is of unrivalled excellence.

The fruit garden, though it produces in abundance, excellent black, white, and red currants, is very inferior in the apples, pears, plums, cherries, gooseberries, and strawberries that it produces, in respect both to size and flavour.

The Lobster, (Cancer grammarus, Lin. syst. Nat.)
on account of its superior excellence, is justly entitled to the first place in the lowest order. Around almost all our rocky shores, these fishes are caught in the summer months, in a depth of water from two to six fathoms, during the night commonly, or, if in the day, only in dark weather. The nets made use of for this purpose are in the form of bags, fixed to iron hoops of about two feet and a half diameter, with pieces of lead to sink them, baited with fish, flesh, or garbage of any kind, which the lobsters devour with the utmost avidity. As soon as they are caught, their claws are bound with twine, to prevent their maiming or killing each other; and they are put into large chests, which are anchored in the water in bays or harbours, where they lye unmolested, till put on board the smacks that carry them, in their wells, alive, weekly, in thousands, to the London market.

Herring, (Clupea harengus)
in the months of July and August, not only pay an annual visit to our coasts, as might have been expected from our situation in the track of the great northern shoal, but enter into and continue for some time in our bays, creeks, and friths; and depart unmolested; as we are either destitute of time, capital, or industry, to avail ourselves of this inexhaustible treasure.

The Coalfish, (Gadus carbonarius)
which is so well known here by the name of the *sellock*, *cuth*, or *seth*, according as the age of it is either one two or more years, is much more abundant than any other,

and, indeed, excels in number almost all the rest of our fish taken together. The fry of this species appear first in May, when they are small in size, and few in number. In August, they increase considerably in both respects; but towards winter, when the seas begin to be stormy, they rush into, and often occupy, most of our bays, in which they are caught in myriads, for their livers, which furnish oil for the lamps, and their fish, that constitutes an extensive and valuable article of food to the poor people.

The Toad, (Rana bufo)
is sometimes seen in the evenings in gardens, and such-like places, crawling but never leaping, as the frog does; and is of an appearance, which, to most people, is not only ugly in the extreme, but even frightful and disgusting. Hence perhaps the opinion that has very generally prevailed, that this reptile is pernicious, and has either by its bite, its saliva, or some other means, sometimes transfused its poison into men, as well as other animals. But this opinion is neither supported by the structure of the animal, as it appears on dissection, nor yet by the instances that are adduced. . . .

The Gannet, (Pelecanus baffanus)
which has here got the name of the *Solan*, or *Soland-goose*, frequents our bays, and fishes in a very peculiar manner. The birds of this species do not breed here; but many of them do on the Stack of Suliskerry, a holm or uninhabited island, a little to the south-west of this country.

The Common Gull, (Larus canus)
our *sea-maw*, or *white-maw*, is so numerous on all our shores, rocks, bays, and harbours, that their noise is sometimes disagreeable.

The Auk, (Alka torda)
the same with our *baukie*, comes hither in March, and
without delay takes possession of almost all the high
rocks on the headlands, where it lays only one large egg
in the shelve of a bare rock, exposed to the heat of the
sun, which probably assists in hatching it.

The Sky-Lark, (Alauda arvensis)
remains with us constantly; it begins to sing about the
first of February, and continues its pleasant notes for
the most part of summer.

The Kestrel, (Falco tinnunculus)
which, from its motion in the air, we name the
windcuffer, may frequently be observed, as if stationed
with its eyes fixed on the ground, to discover its prey,
small birds, mice, and chickens, on which it darts down
with such unerring speed, that they very seldom escape
its talons.

The Ringtail Eagle, (Falco fulvus)
which, together with the other eagles, is here named
the *erne*, is very frequently seen on the hills, builds on
the rocks, is of a large size, distinguished from the rest
by a band of white encompassing the root of the tail,
and the legs being covered with feathers down to the
very feet; and is of such prodigious strength, that it is
sometimes said to have carried from a considerable
distance to its eyry, not only fowls, but lambs, pigs, and
even, in some instances, young children, if we trust the
authority of a respectable author, whose account is also
supported by tradition. . . .

The Otter, (Mustela lutra)
is very frequently found burrowing on the shores of the
sea, and on the banks of fresh-water lochs, where it lives
on cod-fish, conger-eels, and all kinds of trout. It is so
nice in its taste, as only to consume the finer parts,
while it leaves the remainder. The fur, which is
excellent, is the only thing valuable, and, if the animal
be killed in winter, sells for about ten shillings Sterling.

The Seal, (Phoca vitulina)
which is here generally known by the name of *selchy*, is
very common on most of our low shores, but particularly on those of the small holms and remote skerries,
where it is frequently seen reposing and basking in the
sun, in fine calm weather, and where it brings forth its
young. The species in this place is very numerous; and
some of them are so large as to measure eight or nine
feet from the point of the nose to the claws of the hind
legs; and, at the shoulders, they are nearly as much in
circumference. If boats be passing near their haunts,
they seem to discover some curiosity in looking
steadfastly, and listening to the stroke of the oars, the
conversation of the people, or to any noise that is
unusual.

They are valuable for their skins, (of which shoes,
slippers, and covers for trunks and saddles are made),
and for the oil which they furnish. In order to obtain
these very useful articles, the animals are knocked
down with clubs, caught in nets, and shot with
muskets. . . . In some few places, the flesh of the young
seals is used fresh; and both in that state and that of
hams, is said to be tolerable.

The Dog, (Canis familiaris)
here is not remarkable, for the only ones we have, are
the greyhound, kept for catching rabbits; the land and
water spaniel and the pointer, used for the purpose of

carrying and fowling; the mastiff, for guarding ships,
and protecting houses; the terrier, used formerly for
searching out rabbits; some varieties of the lapdog; and
the shepherd's dog, with its mongrels. This faithful
animal is the constant guardian of the corn and the
grass in the fields, as well as of the production of the
gardens, against the whole tribe of domestic grani-
vorous animals. To a little farmer, in a mean condition,
his dog is of even more value than a horse or a cow;
since it is by his means alone that he can preserve the
produce of his possession.

The Sheep, (Ovis aries)
here is a peculiar breed, and, from some features in its
character, seems to have sprung from the same stock
with those of Iceland, the Ferroes, and Shetland.
Though of a tolerably good kind, and every where very
numerous, they are of little benefit to the owners,
owing to the absurd custom of suffering them to run
wild on the extensive commons, exposed to the violence
of the sea, the severity of the weather, the depredation
of various distempers, and to the dogs and eagles. . . .
In some places, the sheep wander to the shore at low-
water, and make a plentiful meal of the different kinds
of sea-weed; and when they have been accustomed to
live much on that food, their flesh is of a dark colour,
dry, and of a coarse texture; and, when prepared for
the table, has been thought to bear some resemblance
to venison. . . .

The North Ronaldsay seaweed-eating sheep

Stones and water and farms, Stenness

For Further Reading

Bailey, Patrick, *Orkney* (Newton Abbot: David & Charles, 1971)

Balfour, E., *Orkney Birds*, Status and Guide (Stromness: C. Senior, 1972)

Brown, George Mackay, *Hawkfall* (London: The Hogarth Press, 1974)

——, *Selected Poems* (London: The Hogarth Press, 1977)

Brown, Malcolm and Meehan, Patricia, *Scapa Flow* (London: Allen Lane, 1968)

Defoe, Daniel, *The Pirate Gow* (Edinburgh: Gordon Wright Publishing, reissued 1978)

Firth, John, *Reminiscences of an Orkney Parish* (Stromness: Orkney Natural History Society, reissued 1974)

Groundwater, William, *Birds and Mammals of Orkney* (Kirkwall: Kirkwall Press, 1974)

Linklater, Eric, *Fanfare for a Tin Hat* (London: Macmillan, 1970)

——, *White-Maa's Saga* (London: Jonathan Cape, 1929)

Marwick, Ernest W., *The Folklore of Orkney and Shetland* (London: Batsford, 1975)

Marwick, Hugh, *Orkney Farm Names* (Kirkwall: W. R. Mackintosh, 1952)

Miller, Ronald, *Orkney* (London: Batsford, 1976)

Muir, Edwin, *An Autobiography* (London: The Hogarth Press, reissued 1980)

——, *Collected Poems* (London: Faber & Faber, 1952)

The New Orkney Book, ed. by J. Shearer (London: Nelson, 1966)

Orkneyinga Saga, trans. by Hermann Pálsson and Paul Edwards (London: The Hogarth Press, 1978)

Rendall, Robert, *Country Sonnets and Other Poems* (Kirkwall: Orcadian Office, n.d.)

——, *The Hidden Land* (Kirkwall: Kirkwall Press, 1966)

——, *Orkney Variants and Other Poems* (Kirkwall: Kirkwall Press, n.d.)

——, *Shore Poems and Other Verse* (Kirkwall: Kirkwall Press, 1957)

Renfrew, Colin, *Investigations in Orkney* (London: Thames & Hudson for the Society of Antiquaries, 1979)

Troup, J. A. and Eunson, F., *Stromness: 150 Years a Burgh, 1817–1967* (Stromness: W. R. Rendall, 1967)